Manal Farrag

Colored Model Based Testing for Software Product Lines

Manal Farrag

Colored Model Based Testing for Software Product Lines

CMBT-SWPL

Südwestdeutscher Verlag für Hochschulschriften

Impressum/Imprint (nur für Deutschland/ only for Germany)
Bibliografische Information der Deutschen Nationalbibliothek: Die Deutsche Nationalbibliothek
verzeichnet diese Publikation in der Deutschen Nationalbibliografie; detaillierte bibliografische
Daten sind im Internet über http://dnb.d-nb.de abrufbar.
Alle in diesem Buch genannten Marken und Produktnamen unterliegen warenzeichen-, marken-
oder patentrechtlichem Schutz bzw. sind Warenzeichen oder eingetragene Warenzeichen der
jeweiligen Inhaber. Die Wiedergabe von Marken, Produktnamen, Gebrauchsnamen,
Handelsnamen, Warenbezeichnungen u.s.w. in diesem Werk berechtigt auch ohne besondere
Kennzeichnung nicht zu der Annahme, dass solche Namen im Sinne der Warenzeichen- und
Markenschutzgesetzgebung als frei zu betrachten wären und daher von jedermann benutzt
werden dürften.

Verlag: Südwestdeutscher Verlag für Hochschulschriften GmbH & Co. KG
Dudweiler Landstr. 99, 66123 Saarbrücken, Deutschland
Telefon +49 681 37 20 271-1, Telefax +49 681 37 20 271-0
Email: info@svh-verlag.de
Zugl.: Ilmenau, TU, Diss., 2010

Herstellung in Deutschland:
Schaltungsdienst Lange o.H.G., Berlin
Books on Demand GmbH, Norderstedt
Reha GmbH, Saarbrücken
Amazon Distribution GmbH, Leipzig
ISBN: 978-3-8381-2388-2

Imprint (only for USA, GB)
Bibliographic information published by the Deutsche Nationalbibliothek: The Deutsche
Nationalbibliothek lists this publication in the Deutsche Nationalbibliografie; detailed
bibliographic data are available in the Internet at http://dnb.d-nb.de.
Any brand names and product names mentioned in this book are subject to trademark, brand
or patent protection and are trademarks or registered trademarks of their respective holders.
The use of brand names, product names, common names, trade names, product descriptions
etc. even without a particular marking in this works is in no way to be construed to mean that
such names may be regarded as unrestricted in respect of trademark and brand protection
legislation and could thus be used by anyone.

Publisher: Südwestdeutscher Verlag für Hochschulschriften GmbH & Co. KG
Dudweiler Landstr. 99, 66123 Saarbrücken, Germany
Phone +49 681 37 20 271-1, Fax +49 681 37 20 271-0
Email: info@svh-verlag.de

Printed in the U.S.A.
Printed in the U.K. by (see last page)
ISBN: 978-3-8381-2388-2

Copyright © 2011 by the author and Südwestdeutscher Verlag für Hochschulschriften GmbH &
Co. KG and licensors
All rights reserved. Saarbrücken 2011

"Quality is never an accident; it is always the result of intelligent effort."
John Ruskin

"Program testing can be used to show the presence of bugs, but never to show their absence!"   Edsger Dijkstra

"A clever person solves a problem. A wise person avoids it."   Albert Einstein

"It is not enough to do your best. You must know what to do and then do your best."   W. Edwards Deming

Zusammenfassung

In den letzten zehn Jahren hat sich die Domäne "Software-Produktlinie" als eins der vielversprechendsten Paradigmen der Softwareentwicklung entwickelt. Die wichtigsten Vorteile eines solchen Ansatzes sind Verbesserungen in Produktivität, Time to Market, Produktqualität und Kundenzufriedenheit.

Um die erforderliche Software-Qualitätssicherung zu erreichen, ist das Testen von Software-Produktlinien von grosser Bedeutung. Das Anliegen dieser Arbeit besteht darin, möglichst früh Tests für Software-Produktlinien zu entwickeln und einzuführen, um Fehler in frühen Phasen zu erkennen. Die Kosten werden demzufolge wesentlich gegenüber dem Erkennen der Fehler in späteren Phasen reduziert.

Die in dieser Arbeit vorgeschlagene Methode ist eine modellbasierte, wiederverwendungsorientierte Testmethode, "Colored Model Based Testing for Software Product Lines" (CMBT-SWPL). CMBT-SWPL ist ein anforderungsbasierter Ansatz für die effiziente Generierung von Tests für Produkte in einer Software-Produktlinie. Dieser Testansatz ist für die Validierung und Verifizierung von Produktlinien vorgesehen. Es ist ein neuartiger Ansatz für Produktlinien-Tests unter Einbeziehung von gefärbten Zustandsdiagrammen (CSCs), wobei die Variabilität in frühen Phasen eines Produktlinienentwicklungsprozesses berücksichtigt wird. Genauer gesagt, wird die Variabilität in die Hauptkomponenten des gefärbten Zustandsdiagramms eingebaut. Dementsprechend wird die Variabilität in den Testfällen aufrechterhalten, welche sich aus dem Testmodell automatisch generieren lassen.

Während des Domain Engineerings wird die CSC aus dem Merkmalmodell abgeleitet. Durch Färbung des State Chart kann das Verhalten mehrerer Varianten von Produktlinien gleichzeitig in einem einzigen Diagramm modelliert werden und somit die Variabilität der Produktlinie früh umgesetzt werden. Das CSC stellt das Testmodell dar, aus der die Testfälle mit Hilfe statistischer Tests abgeleitet werden können.

Während des Application Engineerings werden diese farbigen Testmodelle für eine bestimmte Anwendung der Produktlinie angepasst. Am Ende dieses Testprozesses werden die Testfälle mit Hilfe statistischer Tests generiert und dann ausgeführt. Die Testergebnisse sind dann bereit für die Bewertung. Darüber hinaus wird das CSC zwecks Verifikation und Simulation in Gefärbte Petri Netze (CPN) umgewandelt.

Der wichtigste Vorteil der Anwendung der CMBT-SWPL-Methode ist die Früherkennung von Fehlern in den Anforderungen, z.B wie Unklarheiten, Unvollständigkeit und Redundanz, was sich dann in Einsparungen bei Testaufwand, Zeit, Entwicklungs- und Wartungskosten auswirkt.

Abstract

Over the last decade, the software product line domain has emerged as one of the most promising software development paradigms. The main benefits of a software product line approach are improvements in productivity, time to market, product quality, and customer satisfaction.

Therefore, one topic that needs greater emphasis is testing of software product lines to achieve the required software quality assurance. Our concern is how to test a software product line as early as possible in order to detect errors, because the cost of error detected in early phases is much less compared to the cost of errors when detected later.

The method suggested in this thesis is a model-based, reuse-oriented test technique called Colored Model Based Testing for Software Product Lines (CMBT-SWPL). CMBT-SWPL is a requirements-based approach for efficiently generating tests for products in a software product line. This testing approach is used for validation and verification of product lines. It is a novel approach to test product lines using a Colored State Chart (CSC), which considers variability early in the product line development process. More precisely, the variability will be introduced in the main components of the CSC. Accordingly, the variability is preserved in test cases, as they are generated from colored test models automatically.

During domain engineering, the CSC is derived from the feature model. By coloring the State Chart, the behavior of several product line variants can be modeled simultaneously in a single diagram and thus address product line variability early. The CSC represents the test model, from which test cases using statistical testing are derived.

During application engineering, these colored test models are customized for a specific application of the product line. At the end of this test process, the test cases are generated again using statistical testing, executed and the test results are ready for evaluation. In addition, the CSC will be transformed to a Colored Petri Net (CPN) for verification and simulation purposes.

The main gains of applying the CMBT-SWPL method are early detection of defects in requirements, such as ambiguities incompleteness and redundancy which is then reflected in saving the test effort, time, development and maintenance costs.

Acknowledgments

I would like to express my deepest thanks and sincere gratitude to my supervisor, Prof. Dr.-Ing. habil.Wolfgang Fengler for his insightful guidance, infinite patience, and endless support throughout this work.

"Thank you much more, Than a greeting can say, Because you were thoughtful, In such a nice way!"

Moreover, I would like to deeply thank my supervisor, Prof. Dr.-Ing. Ilka Philipow. Her understanding, encouraging and personal guidance have provided a good basis for the present thesis.

"Gratitude is the memory of the heart. Italian Proverb"

I am deeply grateful to my supervisor Assistant Prof. Dr.-Ahmed Ghoneim, for his support throughout this work.

"Blessed are those who give without remembering. And blessed are those who take without forgetting. Bernard Meltzer"

There is someone I like to thank from the bottom of my heart. Many thanks Prof. Gerd Jäger, you supported and encouraged me and without your guidance I could never reach my goal.

"One can pay back the loan of gold, but one dies forever in debt to those who are kind. Malayan Proverb"

I warmly thank Dr. Detlef Streidtferdt, for his valuable advice and friendly help. His extensive and interesting discussions on my work have been very helpful for this study.

"One of the most beautiful gifts in the world is the gift of encouragement. When someone encourages you, that person helps you over a threshold you might otherwise never have crossed on your own. - John O'Donohue"

In addition, I would like to thank everyone at the Faculty of Computer Science and Automation - Institute of Computer Engineering - Ilmenau University of Technology for their support and help. I would like to extend special thanks to Alexander Fleischer, Heiner Kotula, Patrick Mäder, Olga Fengler, Bernd Däne, Cordula Höring, Sabine Sauerbrey. Note I would have to list the name of everyone in the department to really complete appreciation section. Therefore, please accept my general appreciation for all of you.

"There is nothing better than the encouragement of a good friend. Jean Jacques Rousseau"

I wish to express my warm and sincere thanks to Dr. Fadia Saud Alsaleh, dean of the College for Women, Prince Sultan University, Saudi Arabia. She was the first one, who encouraged me, supported me and facilitated all administrative obstacles in order to travel to Germany and conduct my PhD there. Moreover, my sincere thanks go to Dr. Ahmed Yamani, Rector, and Dr. Abdelhafeez Feda, Vice-Rector of Prince Sultan University, who agreed on giving me a leave to conduct my research.
In addition, I like to deeply thank Dr. Mahmoud Abdel Halim for his great effort and support.

"We don't accomplish anything in this world alone ... and whatever happens is the result of the whole tapestry of one's life and all the weavings of individual threads from one to another that creates something. Sandra Day O'Connor "

Furthermore, I want to thank my family for their loving and tremendous support that made this work possible, and for this I am very thankful and humble.

"My dear dad, mom and sister, I only kept going because of your encouragement"

My children, Layla, Yousra, Ahmed and my family in law fully supported me.

"Thank you for your love and patience; I love you from the bottom of my heart"

Last but not least, I would like to thank my dear husband. His love and support without any complaint or regret has enabled me to complete this PhD. Being both a father and a mother while I was away was not an easy task. I owe him every achievement.

"It's amazing how two words that mean so much can seem so little. If I could show you how much your presence in my life means to me, the simple phrase of 'thank you' would pale and diminish in the sheer enormity of the gratitude I owe."

Thank you all – I could not have done this alone.

I thank God for you

Contents

Zusammenfassung		iii
Abstract		v
Acronyms		xvii

1 Introduction   1
    1.1 Motivation and Scope of Research 1
    1.2 Product Line's System Testing Challenges 4
    1.3 Contribution of Thesis 6
    1.4 Layout of the Study 7
    1.5 Research Area 8

2 State of the Art   9
    2.1 Software Product Line 9
       2.1.1 Software Reuse 9
       2.1.2 Software Product Lines' Terminologies 11
       2.1.3 Typical Examples of Software Product Lines 13
       2.1.4 The Software Product Line Paradigm 14
       2.1.5 Variability 18
       2.1.6 Feature & Feature Modelling 19
    2.2 Software Product Line Testing 21
       2.2.1 Introduction 21
       2.2.2 Colored Model Based Testing for Software Product Lines (CMBT-SWPL) 23
       2.2.3 Scenario based TEst Derivation(ScenTED) 25
       2.2.4 Customizable Activity Diagrams, Decision Tables and Test Specifications(CADeT) 27
       2.2.5 Related Work for Software Product Line Testing 29

		2.2.6	State-based Software Product Line Testing	31
		2.2.7	Testing Strategies for Software Product Lines	31

3 Fundamentals 35

3.1 Quality Assurance and Testing 35

    3.1.1 Introduction 35

    3.1.2 Computer System Failures caused by Software Bugs 36

    3.1.3 Reasons for Bugs in Software 39

    3.1.4 Different Definitions for Testing 39

    3.1.5 Difference between Quality Assurance, Quality Control and Testing 41

    3.1.6 Debugging and Testing 43

    3.1.7 How Testing should be? 44

    3.1.8 The Test Process 45

    3.1.9 Purpose of Testing 45

    3.1.10 Testing Principles 46

    3.1.11 Software Testing Types 47

    3.1.12 Comparison between Black-Box Testing & White-Box Testing . . . 50

3.2 Unified Modeling Language(UML) 51

    3.2.1 Building Models 51

    3.2.2 Visual Modeling 52

    3.2.3 UML 53

    3.2.4 UML Definition 53

    3.2.5 Diagrams overview 54

3.3 Petri Nets (PNs) and Colored Petri Nets (CPNs) 54

    3.3.1 Petri Nets (PNs) 54

    3.3.2 Colored Petri Nets (CPNs) 57

    3.3.3 CPN-Graphical Representation 57

    3.3.4 CPN-Formal Representation 58

    3.3.5 CPN and Simulation 58

    3.3.6 CPN and Verification 59

3.4	State Charts and Colored State Charts	59
	3.4.1 State Charts	59
	3.4.2 Colored State Chart(CSC)	65
3.5	Embedded Systems	65
	3.5.1 Introduction to Embedded Systems	65
	3.5.2 Embedded Systems Characteristics	66
	3.5.3 Reactive Embedded Systems	67

4 Main Requirements of Colored Model Based Testing for Software Product Lines Method   69

4.1	CMBT-SWPL Method's Requirements	69
4.2	Summary	72

5 Case Study : Universal Remote Control(URC)   75

5.1	Introduction	75
5.2	Universal Remote Control	76
5.3	Universal Remote Control-Feature Model	78

6 Main Aspects for Applying the Colored Model Based Testing for Software Product Lines Method   83

6.1	Introduction	83
6.2	The W-Model for Testing Software Product Lines	83
6.3	Model Based Testing	86
	6.3.1 Model Based Testing Steps	88
	6.3.2 Benefits of Model-Based Testing (MBT)	89
6.4	Model-Based Statistical Testing	89
	6.4.1 Statistical Usage Testing	90
	6.4.2 Phases of Statistical Testing	92
	6.4.3 Statistical Testing using JUMBL	92
	6.4.4 Test Generation using JUMBL	94
6.5	State Charts (SCs)	94

6.6	Why State Charts?	95
	6.6.1 Why not Natural Language Specifications?	96
	6.6.2 Advantages of State Charts	96

7 Colored Model Based Testing for Software Product Lines (CMBT-SWPL) — 99

7.1	Introduction	99
7.2	Colored State Charts (CSCs)	99
	7.2.1 Example: Folding of States and Transitions	100
	7.2.2 Formal Definitions	101
7.3	Testing Product Lines with CMBT-SWPL Method	103
	7.3.1 CMBT-SWPL : Domain Engineering.	103
	7.3.2 CMBT-SWPL : Application Engineering	115
	7.3.3 Statistical Testing	117
7.4	Colored Petri Nets (CPN)	121
7.5	PENECA Chromos	121
7.6	Simulation	121

8 Evaluation — 127

8.1	Introduction	127
8.2	Results	127
8.3	Colored Model Based Testing for Software Product Lines - Strong Points	128
8.4	Discussion	130

9 Conclusion — 133

9.1	Summary of the Thesis's Layout	133
9.2	CMBT-Method in a Nutshell	134
9.3	Suggested Studies	135

Synonymic Terminologies 137

Glossary 139

List of Figures 149

List of Tables	**153**
Bibliography	**165**
Index	**169**

Acronyms

ANSI	American National Standards Institute	
BFS	Brute Force Strategy	
CADeT	Customizable Activity Diagrams, Decision Tables and Test Specifications	
CMBT-SWPL	Colored Model Based Testing for Software Product Lines	
CPN	Colored Petri Net	
CRS	Commonality and Reuse Strategy	
CSC	Colored State Chart	
CSV	Comma-Separated Value	
DLLs	Dynamic Link Libraries	
DVB	Digital Video Broadcasting	
DVP	Digital Video Project	
e.g.	Latin: exempli gratia (for example)	
ES	Embedded Systems	
FeatuRSEB	Feature Reuse-driven Software Engineering Business	
FM	Feature Model	
FODA	Feature-Oriented Domain Analysis	
FORM	Feature-Oriented Reuse Method	
FSM	Finite State Machines	

i.e.	Latin: id est (that is); (in other words); (that is to say)
IEEE	Institute of Electrical and Electronics Engineers
IR	InfraRed
IrDA	Infrared Data Association
IT	Information Technology
JUMBL	Java Usage Model Builder Library
MBT	Model Based Testing
MML	Model Markup Language
MPEG	Motion Picture Encoding Group
OCL	Object Constraint Language
OMG	Object Management Group
OO	Object-Oriented
PAS	Pure Application Strategy
PL	Product Line
PLSE	Product Line Software Engineering
PLUC	Product Line Use Case
PLUS	Product Line UML-Based Software Engineering
PLUTO	Product Line Use case Test Optimization
QA	Quality Assurance
QC	Quality Control
RUP	Rational Unified Process
SAS	Sample Application Strategy
SC	State Chart

Technical University of Ilmenau

ScenTED	Scenario based TEst case Derivation
SE	Software Engineering
SPL	Software Product Line
SPLE	Software Product Line Engineering
SQRL	Software Quality Research Laboratory
Std	Standard
SUT	System Under Test
TDD	Test Driven Development
TML	The Model Language
UML	Unified Modeling Language
URC	Universal Remote Control
VCR	Videocassette Recorder
VDR	Video Disk Recorder

Chapter 1

Introduction

'"Whatever you can do or dream, begin it."' Johann Wolfgang von Goethe (1749 - 1832)

1.1 Motivation and Scope of Research

The product line approach to software development is based on the systematic, large scale reuse of development artifacts such as architecture, design, and components among a set of functionally similar products. It promises, among other things, to shorten the development time of software systems and to significantly reduce development and maintenance costs. The software product line development is presented in the following table 1.1:

Domain Engineering (Development for Reuse)	Application Engineering (Development with Reuse)
During the domain engineering, reusable artifacts are produced.	During application engineering, applications are built from these artifacts to create customer specific applications.

Table 1.1: Software Product Lines Development

Research in the field of software product lines to date has focused primarily on analysis, design, and implementation. In particular, the quality assurance challenges that arise in a product line context have been addressed insufficiently so far, and there is little guidance for product line organizations on how to systematically assure the quality of their product lines and reusable artifacts.[KM04]

To achieve the promised improvements, however, the components and artifacts intended for reuse must be of high quality since the components are potentially reused in many family members. Thus a defect (figure 1.1) in one of the components or even in the core of the family has effects on many delivered products and carries the risk of very high costs to solve such defects. Thus, more than for traditional software development, testing becomes a very crucial part of every product line effort.

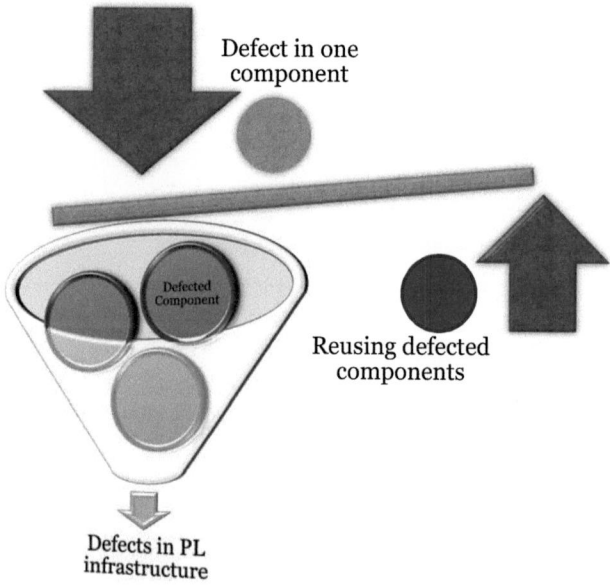

Figure 1.1: Defected components and their influence on PL infrastructure

Therefore, the emphasis (figure 1.2) in this thesis is on testing software product lines as early as possible in order to reduce the test effort and development and maintenance costs targeting a competitive advantage in the market.

Each software development paradigm requires a suitable test model. Accordingly, soft-

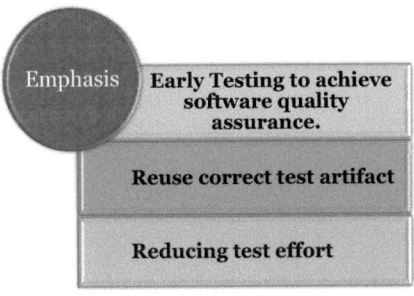

Figure 1.2: Thesis's Emphasis

ware product line engineering needs also an appropriate test model to complete the whole product engineering.[JHQJ08]

The main challenge for testing is how to deal adequately with both the separation of product lines into domain engineering and application engineering and the presence of variability. [PBvdL05]

This thesis suggests a new system test method for software product lines, the **Colored Model Based Testing for Software Product Lines (CMBT-SWPL)**, based on Colored State Charts. It describes two separate and closely related sub-models of domain test and application test.

In the next section, the main challenges that face system testing in product lines are discussed in more detail.

1.2 Product Line's System Testing Challenges

Main challenges, problems and obstacles (figure 1.3) that face system testing in the product line paradigm are presented briefly:

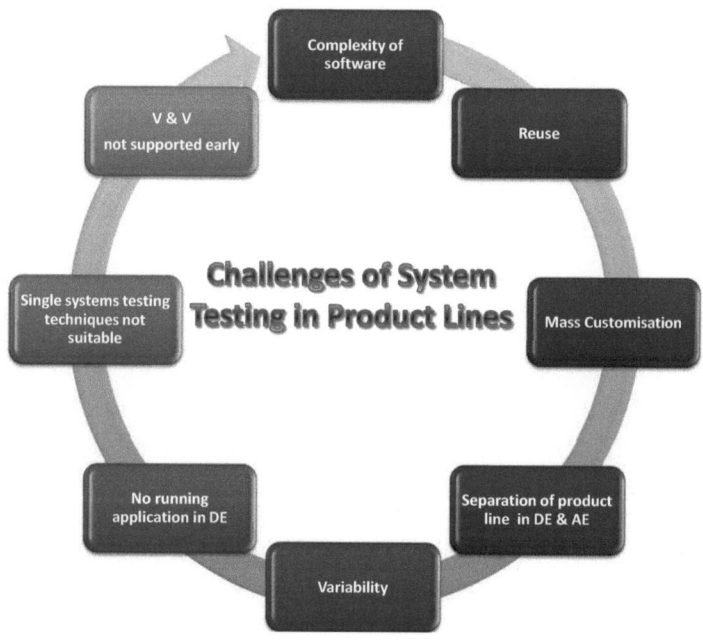

Figure 1.3: Challenges of System Testing in Product Lines

1. Software is becoming complex.

2. The software product line paradigm focuses on mass customization, which is the ability to efficiently create many variations of a product. It is a big advance in both manufacturing and software engineering. The key to mass customization is to capitalize on the commonality and to effectively manage the variation in a product line. Therefore, producing goods and services to meet individual customer's needs should be done with the utmost mass production efficiency.

3. Reuse is essential.

   However, reuse is double-edged: it scales up everything, including the consequences of possible flaws. Then, quality becomes critical. Without quality, the dangers of reusing components may well offset the advantages. Therefore, reuse must be dealt with care.

4. The main challenge for testing is how to deal adequately with the separation of product line into domain engineering and application engineering.

5. The next challenge testing is facing is that, in the domain engineering, there is no running application. We can only test components or integrated chunks of data. The applications are available only in application testing.

6. The presence of variability in product lines is another challenge. In an ideal world, it is desired to test every possible combination in an application. However, in most cases, this simply is not possible, due to the number of possible inputs, combinations of features and configurations, and paths through the code. A simple application can have hundreds or thousands of possible input and output combinations. "Creating test cases for all of these possibilities is impractical. Complete testing of a complex application would take too long and require too many human resources to be economically feasible." [Mye04]

7. The testing techniques used in single systems can not be directly applied in product lines. They must be adapted to suit the nature of product lines.

8. Early Validation and Verification is not fully supported. Many testing techniques are performed late, when there is a running application. Thus a defect in one of the components or even in the core of the family has effects on many delivered products and poses the risk of very high costs to solve such defects.

1.3 Contribution of Thesis

The goal of this thesis is to establish an efficient overall testing process using the CMBT-SWPL method in order to overcome the problems and obstacles mentioned above. Testing aspects have to be considered right from the beginning of the development to ensure that requirements and design support testing.

The method (figure 1.4) should facilitate the following:

- Providing reusable test artifacts.
- Early Validation and Verification.
- An appropriate test model that can represent the product line variants in a compact way and cope with the software product line engineering challenges.
- Systematic test case generation.
- Reducing development and maintenance effort and cost.

Section 1.5 shows the main research area on which the method is built. On the other hand, chapter 4 discusses the main requirements for the CMBT-SWPL method in more details.

It is worthy of note that the domain of interest is an embedded product line. Therefore, a suitable test model to represent the behavior of the embedded product line should be selected. The behavioral test model chosen, was the Colored State Chart (CSC). The idea of colored models has been originally examined before by [FFDD02][FFD02][Fen04]. It has been performed for real-time complex systems. The idea was adjusted to suit testing an embedded product line system of a Universal Remote Control (URC). Furthermore, the CSC is used to systematically generate test cases. The thesis shows how the new feature, "'color"', was incorporated into the existing rules.

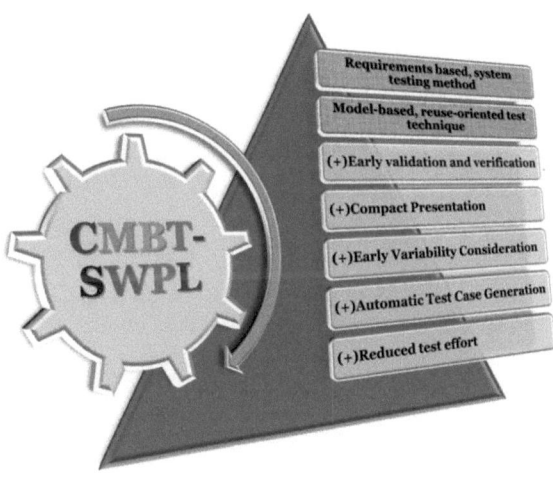

Figure 1.4: CMBT-SWPL Method

1.4 Layout of the Study

This thesis is organized as follows. Chapter 1 introduces challenges facing system testing, contribution of the thesis as well as research area on which the test method is built. Chapter 2 is an extensive study of software product lines and product line testing. Fundamentals in Quality Assurance, Testing, Petri Nets, Colored Petri Nets, State Charts, Colored State Charts and embedded reactive systems are presented in chapter 3. Chapter 4 discusses the main requirements of CMBT-SWPL method. Chapter 5 demonstrates the case study used for the description and evaluation of the methodology developed in this work. The main aspects for applying the CMBT-SWPL method are presented in chapter 6. Chapter 7 introduces the details of the proposed methodology "Colored Model Based Testing for Software Product Lines (CMBT-SWPL)". Respectively and finally, chapter 8 and 9 evaluate and summarize this work.

1.5 Research Area

The following figure 1.5 demonstrates the research area of this thesis.

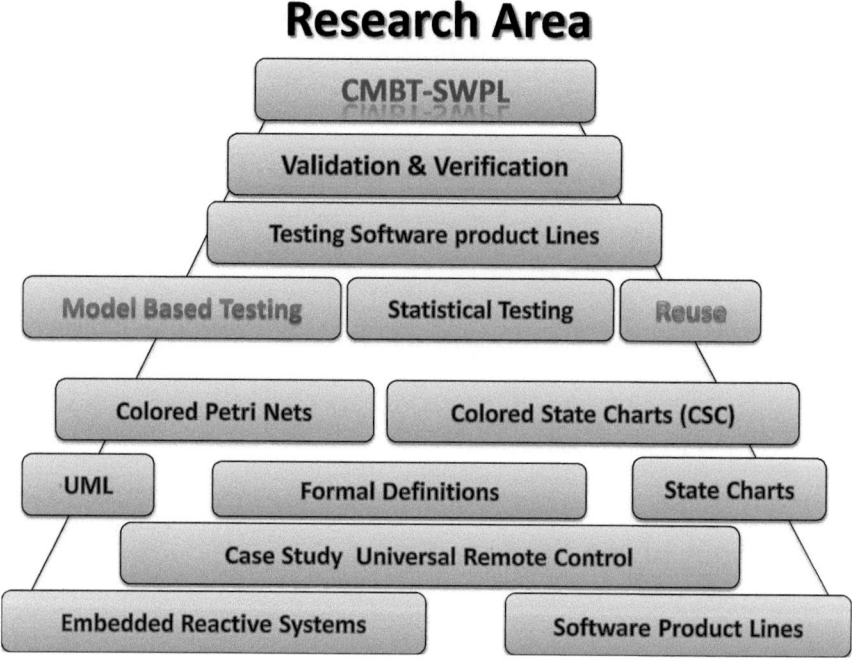

Figure 1.5: Research Area

Chapter 2

State of the Art

"What keeps me going is goals." Muhammad Ali

2.1 Software Product Line

This chapter is mainly a state of the art study of software product lines and software product line testing. Software reuse at the beginning emphasizes that in order to apply the product line concept, planned strategic reuse should be targeted. Next, the software product line paradigm is presented with its different terminologies, examples, subprocesses, variability, features and feature modeling and promised, if applied correctly, considerable benefits in terms of reduced costs, shortened time-to market and increased product quality. Moreover, section 2.1 demonstrates our own developed product line reference process used in this thesis to introduce the development artifacts in parallel to the test artifacts for the different test approaches relevant to our domain of interest. Section 2.2. starts with demonstrating the three main approaches for testing product lines, namely CMBT-SWPL, ScenTED and CADeT and ends with listing related work in testing software product lines followed by the main state-based approaches for testing software product lines. The chapter ends with demonstrating the different testing strategies for software product lines.

2.1.1 Software Reuse

The dream of massive software reuse is as old as software engineering itself[vdLSR07]. From subroutines in the 1960s through modules in the 1970s, objects in the 1980s, and components in the 1990s, software engineering has been the story of a continuously ascending spiral of increasing capability and economy battled by increasing complexity(figure 2.1). Numerous attempts to reuse software were made, but usually with little success. These

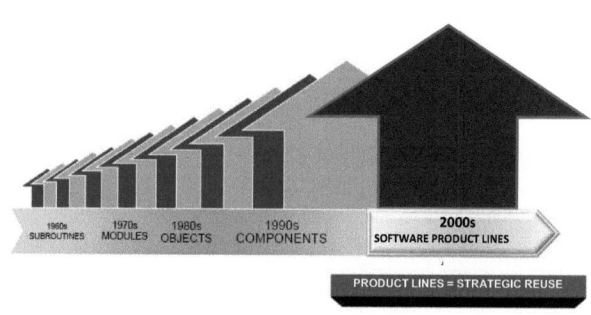

Figure 2.1: Reuse History (adjusted after [Nor08])

reuse initiatives were usually based on an approach focusing on small-scale and ad hoc reuse (typically on the code-level - or at least within a development phase). Software reuse has been one of the goals in software engineering since 1968, when the term software engineering was first coined. Traditional approaches to software reuse have proved ineffective in addressing the software crisis in practice. Now at the dawn of the new millennium, comes the next great turn of the cycle. The field of software reuse has evolved from the reuse of individual components toward the large-scale reuse with software product lines. [Gom04][vdLSR07] Studies have shown that organizations can yield remarkable improvements in productivity, time to market, product quality and customer satisfaction by applying this approach.[Eri03]

Reuse Definition:

"Reuse is the process of implementing or updating software systems using existing software assets. Assets can be specifications, design, code, user documentation, or anything associated with software. Reuse is an integral part of every engineering discipline."[Jor97]

Reuse Benefits

Expected benefits of reusability are numerous; it should [Mey00]:

- Improve timeliness (in the sense of bringing your product faster to market);
- Decrease maintenance effort (since it is not the programmer's duty anymore, but the duty of the software provider);
- Increase reliability (by relying on components produced by well-known, reputed third parties);
- Boost efficiency (since developers can reuse the algorithms and data structures that best fit their needs);
- Lead to better consistency of the software design (since programmers are likely to apply the same design rules as the ones conveyed by the libraries they reuse);
- Help preserve the know-how of the best developers by contributing this fragile resource to a well of permanent assets.

2.1.2 Software Product Lines' Terminologies

This part presents software product lines as an approach to software reuse. Software product line is a new paradigm that aims to reduce the development time and cost and increase software quality. This reduction is achieved by reusing software artifacts in a systematic and proactive way, not like the previous traditional opportunistic reuse way (table 2.1). The traditional opportunistic reuse way was based on putting general software components into a library in the hope that opportunities for reuse will occur. on the other, hand software product lines are based on proactive reuse, which is a planned strategic reuse. "It is important to realize that a software product line never happen by accident. For any software reuse initiative to be successful, it has to be a carefully planed and enforced activity."[Eri03]

Previous Efforts	Software Product Lines
Opportunistic Software Reuse	Proactive Software Reuse

Table 2.1: Proactive versus Opportunistic Software Reuse

The following definitions are fundamental to understand the concept of software product line([PBvdL05]):

The classic definition for a software product line is:

"A software product line is a set of software-intensive systems that share a common, managed set of features satisfying the specific needs of a particular market segment or mission and that are developed from a common set of core assets in a prescribed way. [CN01]"

Platform Definitions:

"A platform is any base of technologies on which other technologies or processes are built."

"A platform is, in the software context, a collection of reusable artifacts."

Mass Customisation Definition:

"Mass customisation is the large-scale production of goods tailored to individual customer's needs."

Domain Engineering Definition:

"Domain engineering is the process of software product line engineering in which the commonality and the variability of the product line are defined and realised."

Application Engineering Definition:

"Application engineering is the process of software product line engineering in which the applications of the product line are built by reusing domain artifacts and exploiting the product line variability."

2.1.3 Typical Examples of Software Product Lines

The idea of a product line is not new. There are examples of product lines in ancient history; the pyramids of Egypt (figure 2.2 on page 13) might have been the first product line! A modern example of product lines comes from the airline industry, with the European Airbus A-318, A-319, A 320, and A-321 airplanes, which share common product features, including jet engines, navigation equipment, and communication equipment[Gom04]. Other examples of companies applying product lines are as diverse as Boeing, Ford and McDonalds[Eri03].

Figure 2.2: A product line from ancient history: The pyramids of Egypt[Gom04]

2.1.4 The Software Product Line Paradigm

The interest in software product lines emerged from the field of software reuse when developers realized that they could obtain much greater reuse benefits by reusing software architectures instead of reusing individual software components. [Gom04]

The software product line engineering paradigm is divided into two processes: the domain engineering and the application engineering processes.

Domain Engineering:

During domain engineering:(see figure 2.3) [vdLSR07] reusable artifacts are produced to create a product platform that can be used as a common baseline for all products within a product family; i.e. the core assets are built for all members of the product line. The core assets are the artifacts used in the development of the product line such as requirement, design, implementation and test artifacts. The domain engineering process itself is further divided into 4 sub-processes: domain requirements engineering, domain design, domain realisation and domain testing (table 2.2) (Terms are defined in the Glossary on page 139).

Domain Engineering Development Process:	
Sub-process	Artifacts produced = core assets
1. Domain Requirements Engineering	Common features & the variability of a product line
2. Domain Design	A reference architecture
3. Domain Realisation	Generic components
4. Domain Testing	Domain test artifacts

Table 2.2: Domain Engineering Process

Application Engineering: On the other hand, the application engineering[vdLSR07] is also divided into 4 sub-processes: application requirements engineering, application design, application realisation and application testing (table 2.3) (Terms are defined in the Glossary on page 139). The core assets, or artifacts, are reused to build a sequence of applications. The different applications are each customized, or tailored, to the needs of the specific customers or stakeholders by selecting different combinations of features from among those

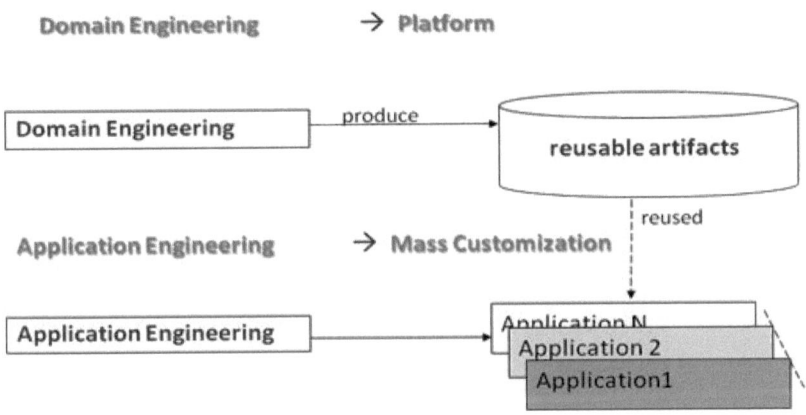

Figure 2.3: Platform versus Mass Customization

defined in the domain-engineering of the product line. Each of these applications, built using the product-line assets (what Gomaa [Gom04] calls the product-line repository), is a member of the product line [Lut07]. To conclude, in application engineering customer-specific applications are built by binding the variability and reusing the domain artifacts. Any unsatisfied requirements (see figure 2.4), errors and adaptations are sent back to the

Application Engineering Development Process:	
Sub-process	Artifacts produced
1. Application Requirements Engineering	Application requirements specification
2. Application Design	Application architecture
3. Application Realisation	A running application
4. Application Testing	Application test artifacts

Table 2.3: Application Engineering Process

domain engineering to perform any required changes on the reusable assets and then they are stored again in the repository. The process of updating the reusable assets, selecting features, deriving and testing each application is repeated until the applications are ready to be delivered to the customers.[Oli08]

Figure 2.4 is the Product Line Engineering Reference Process which the author has developed as a reference process in order to compare the different test methods that are going to be added later to this model. This reference process was influenced by Klaus Pohl's [PBvdL05], Gomaa's [Gom04] frameworks. In figure 2.4 we can see various standard development artifacts that are going to be extended with the various test artifacts for each approach including our own colored approach (CMBT-SWPL).

Therefore, this work is keen to demonstrate the test development method suggested in parallel to the development phase and similarly into two test processes like the domain engineering process and the application engineering process. Thus figure 2.4 will be extended to express the different as well as suggested test methods demonstrated in figure 2.5, which facilitates comparing the main different test methods dealing with testing software product lines in the literature.

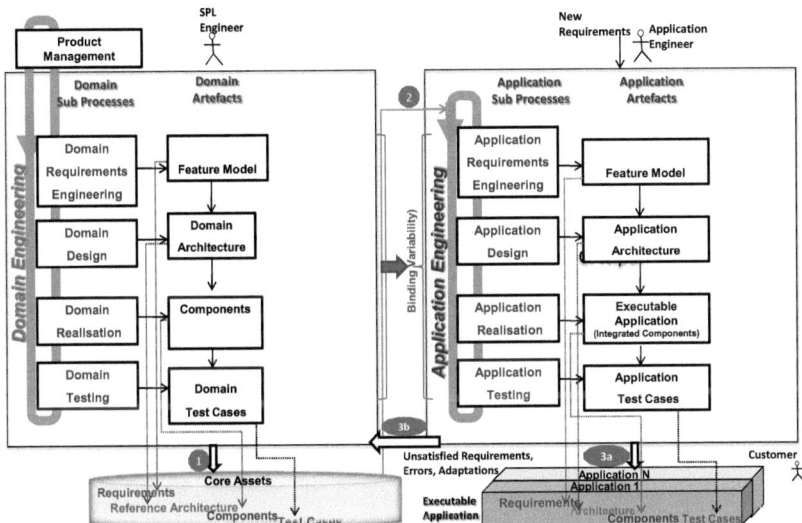

Figure 2.4: Product Line Engineering Reference Process

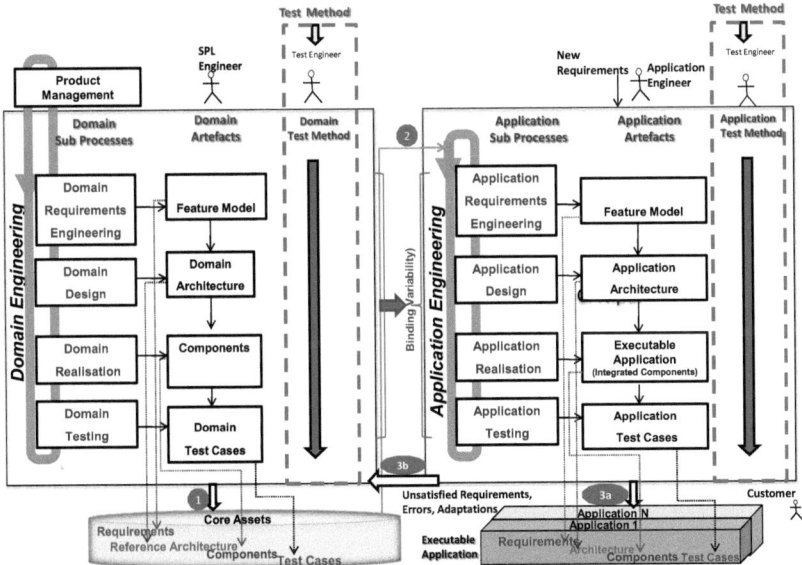

Figure 2.5: Test Method Extended Product Line Engineering Reference Process

2.1.5 Variability

Software product lines support product diversification (figure 2.6), which means that the software is prepared for change by identifying the commonalities and variabilities within a family of products. Variability is defined as the ability of a software system or artifact to be efficiently extended, changed, customized or configured for use in a particular context. Variability is often expressed in the form of so-called variation points. A variation point typically has an associated set of variants (options). A variant is first introduced (made explicit) and then bound (selected) at a specific phase (moment) during the development or deployment process, e.g., at run-time. Examples of variants may range from parameter types, source code constructs and functions to components, Dynamic Link Libraries (DLLs) and stand-alone subprograms. A variation point can be seen as an explicit placeholder in the product line architecture that accommodates product specific functionality in the form of variants.[JKB08]

Most Product Lines offer more potential variability than is in use at any one time, and testing all possible variants is usually impossible and in some cases considered a waste of time. Testing just those variants produced is already a difficult problem where there is a high number of variants. Because of this variability, testing a product Line also represents a significant challenge.

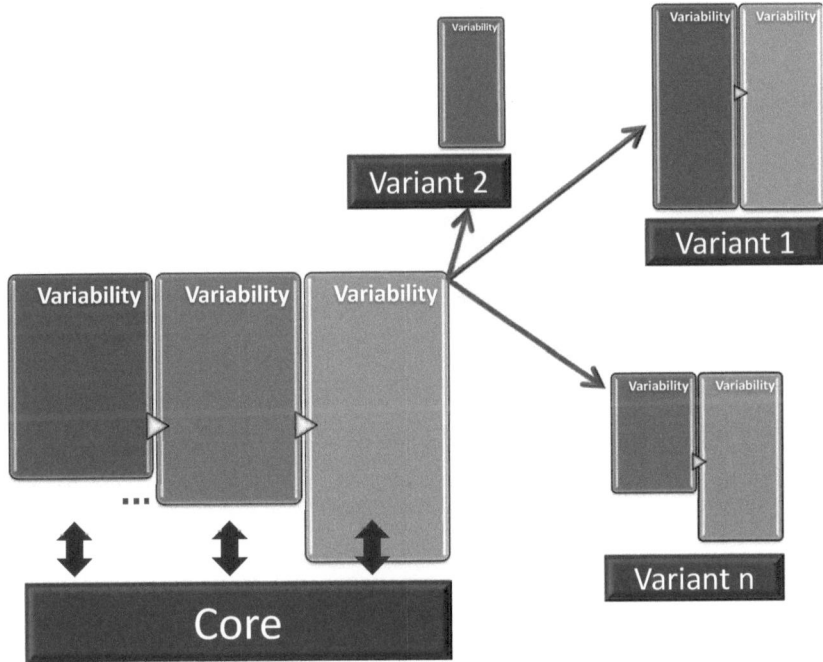

Figure 2.6: Software Product Lines support Product Diversification

2.1.6 Feature & Feature Modelling

The traditional mode of software development is to develop single systems-that is, to develop each system individually. To model and design families of systems, the analysis and design concepts for single product systems need to be extended to support software product lines. For software product lines, the development approach is broadened to consider a family of software systems. This approach involves analyzing what features (functional requirements) of the software family are common, optional, and alternative. After feature analysis, the goal is to design a software architecture for the product line, which has common components (required by all members of the family), optional components (required by only some members of the family), and variant components (different versions of which are required by different members of the family). Instead of going back to square one, the developer derives applications by adapting and tailoring the product line architecture[Gom04]. The following two definitions from [Bos00] and [Rie03] were combined into the following feature definition.

> "Features are a logical unit of behavior that is specified by a set of functional and quality requirements and represent an aspect valuable to the customer."

From a set of features, a software product line can be generated that shares common features and differs in other features [AK10]. In particular, features are characteristics used to differentiate between members of the product line and hence identify the common and variable functionality of a software product line.

The feature concept is not an object oriented one, and it is not used in UML modeling of single systems. [Gom04] Features may be structured in feature models. These are hierarchical tree illustrations of features. Feature models describe the system family in an early stage of the development cycle and are used to specify members of a product-line. To sum up, features may serve as a means of [SPH04]:

- modeling large domains
- managing the variability of PL products
- encapsulating system requirements
- guiding the PL development
- driving marketing decisions
- future planning
- communication between system stakeholders

2.2 Software Product Line Testing

2.2.1 Introduction

System testing of a product line has the same goal as testing of a single system, which is checking the quality of software systems. The test methods applied in single systems can not be directly used in testing the product line. They have to be adapted, and new testing techniques have to be developed. Thus, testing in product lines requires a more efficient test approach than testing in a single system. The main challenge for domain testing is how to deal adequately with both the separation between domain engineering and application engineering and the presence of variability.

Although reuse is a core concept in software product line development, testing does not yet fully benefit from reuse. If delayed and not treated properly, testing can become a serious bottleneck in product line development[Met06]. Therefore, the idea of proactive reuse should be extended to product line testing [RKPR05].

As depicted in (figure 2.4) and in (figure 2.5) the Product Line Engineering Reference Process suggested here, which represents the two phases of development the product line development phase called the domain engineering phase and the product development phase called the application engineering phase, will be extended with a testing method as it is performed in the development [JHQJ08]. Accordingly, test development for the product line should be done in the two phases of domain engineering and in application engineering respectively.

Reusing test artifacts and **model based testing** are the two main aspects (figure 2.7) taken into consideration when comparing (figure 2.8) the different approaches dealing with software product line testing[RKPR05].

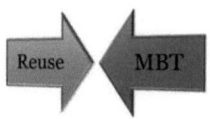

Figure 2.7: Reuse and MBT - Aspects of comparison

Approaches	Reuse	MBT
McGregor 2001 & Geppert et al. 2004	YES	NO
Nebut et al. 2006	YES	NO
Hartmann et al. 2004	NO	YES
Bertolino and Gnesi 2006	YES	NO
ScenTED 2005	YES	YES
CADeT 2008	YES	YES
CMBT 2010	YES	YES

Figure 2.8: Comparison on Supporting Reuse Or/And Model Based Testing

The next three subsections demonstrate the three main approaches for testing product lines, namely CMBT-SWPL, ScenTED and CADeT. Section 2.2 ends with listing related work in testing software product lines followed by the main state-based approaches for testing software product lines. At the end, the different testing strategies for software product lines are explained and compared.

2.2.2 Colored Model Based Testing for Software Product Lines (CMBT-SWPL)

The Colored Model-Based Testing for Software Product Lines (CMBT-SWPL)(figure 2.9), which is a model based, reuse-oriented technique, is our contribution regarding testing product lines. It is a new requirements based system testing method used for validation and verification of product lines. The CMBT-SWPL approach is explained in more detail under section 7.3 (see page 103).

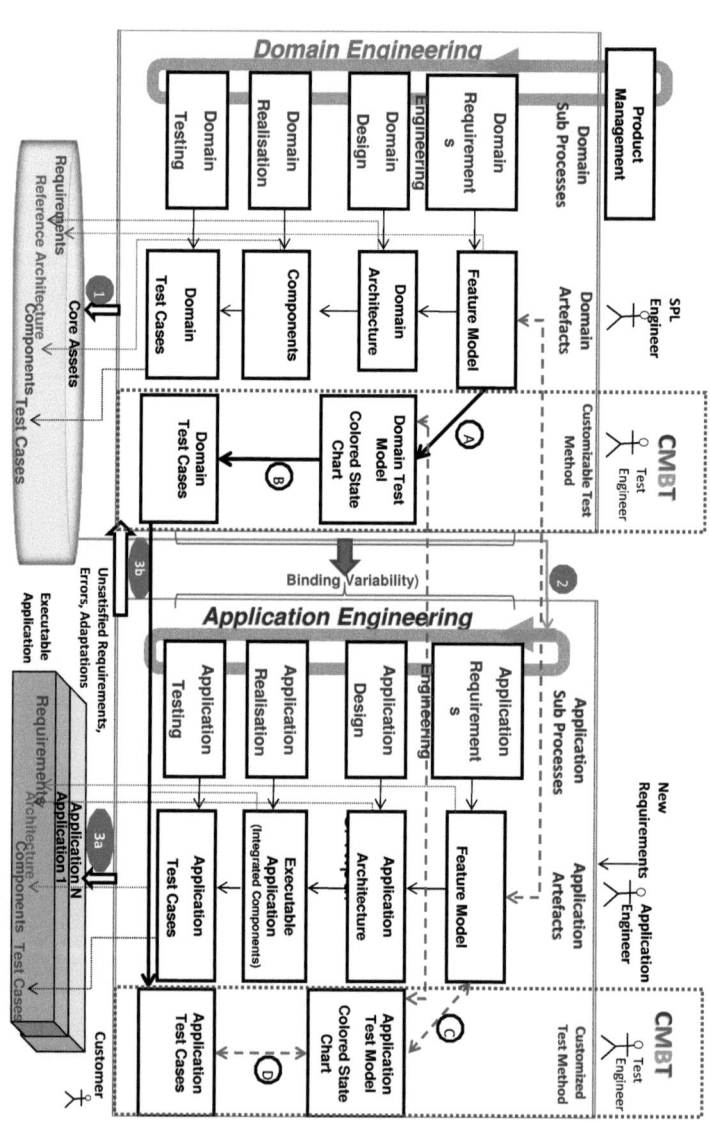

Figure 2.9: Colored Model-Based Testing for Software Product Lines (CMBT-SWPL)

2.2.3 Scenario based TEst Derivation(ScenTED)

As depicted in figure 2.10, the ScenTED technique (Scenario based TEst case Derivation) aims at reducing effort in product family testing. ScenTED is a model-based, reuse-oriented technique for test case derivation in the system test of software product families.

The ScenTED technique is based on the assumption that requirements have been specified as use cases. Thus, during activity A (the left part of figure 2.10) requirements specified in use cases are modeled as domain activity diagram containing variability. Activity diagrams are used as test model from which test case scenarios are derived. During activity B (the left part of figure 2.10) in domain engineering test case scenarios are derived using an adapted coverage criterion for product family engineering. The test case scenarios are specified in sequence diagrams. Test case scenarios describe the test engineer's actions and the responses of the system without specifying concrete test data. Activity C (the right part of figure 2.10) comprises the adaptation of these test case scenarios for a customer-specific application. Traceability information (depicted by the dotted arrows) created during the first two activities is required to perform activity C.

(ScenTED) technique was applied to an industrial case study at Siemens. A test engineer uses ScenTED to create hierarchical activity diagrams from the use cases of an SPL, and then uses the "variant" stereotype to identify decision nodes and activities in the activity diagrams that correspond to variation points. The test engineer uses ScenTED to trace paths from the activity diagrams during SPL engineering to satisfy the branch coverage testing criterion, and then convert these paths to test specifications, which can be manually customized for an application derived from the software product line.

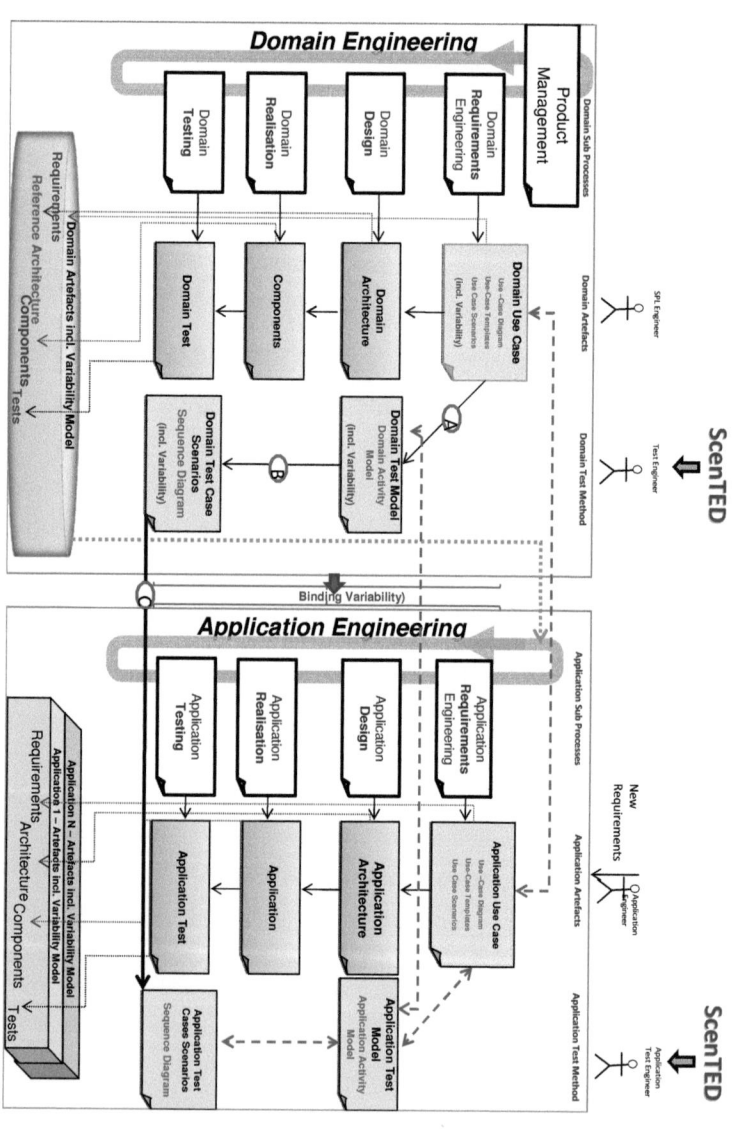

Figure 2.10: ScenTED (Scenario based TEst Derivation)

2.2.4 Customizable Activity Diagrams, Decision Tables and Test Specifications(CADeT)

As depicted in figure 2.11, the CADeT Approach, (Customizable Activity Diagrams, Decision Tables and Test Specifications) is a feature-oriented model-based functional test design method for software product lines. CADeT is incorporated within the Product Line UML-Based Software Engineering(PLUS) method described in [Gom04]. CADeT extends PLUS to create activity diagrams and decision tables from the use case and feature models of a Software Product Line (SPL). The decision tables are used to generate reusable, functional system test specifications for a SPL. During SPL engineering, PLUS is used to create feature and use case requirements models, and CADeT is used to develop customizable activity diagrams, decision tables, and test specifications from these models. During application engineering, PLUS is used to derive one or more applications from the SPL, and CADeT is used to select and customize the test specifications for each application. Each derived application is then tested using the test specifications derived using the same feature model.

In CAdeT, SPL Test Modeling consists of creating activity diagrams from use cases to provide greater precision in the use case descriptions, creating decision tables to formalize the test specifications, and defining a feature based test plan that provides test coverage of all use case scenarios, all features, and selected feature combinations of a SPL. Feature-based Test Derivation consists of deriving the test specifications for the derived application, selecting the test data, and testing the application.[OG09]

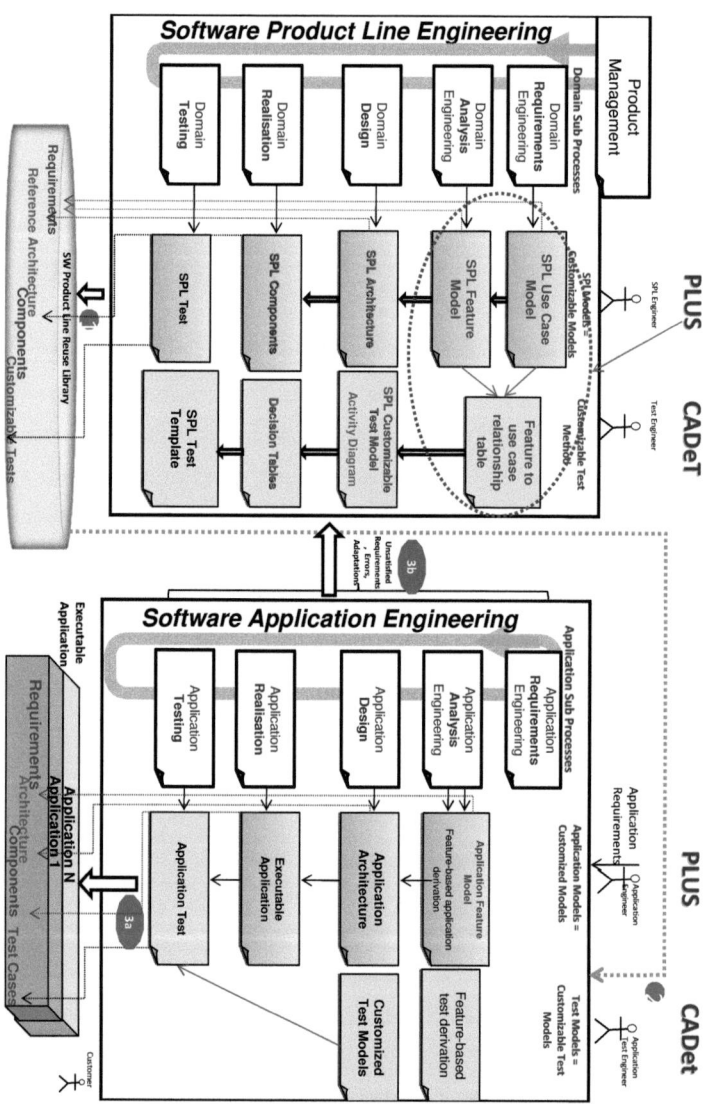

Figure 2.11: Evolutionary Software Product Line Engineering Process merged with CADeT

2.2.5 Related Work for Software Product Line Testing

Table 2.4 and table 2.5 represent related work in Software Product Line Testing.

McGregor [McG01]	McGregor et al. discusses the overall issues for product line testing and assumes that product line test development starts from requirements. McGregor developed a testing process for the requirements-based testing of core assets and applications of a software product line. This process described how test management activities, requirements-based testing strategies, and test specifications could be adapted to fit within a software product line development process. He points out the importance of a well-defined process for testing software product lines.
Kolb [Kol03]	Kolb discusses the challenges facing testing software product lines and highlights some problems particular to testing software product lines, such as reusing generic tests and test results, and choosing which variants to test from a potentially large number of variants. He outlines an approach that helps testing product lines more effectively and efficiently.
Bertolino and Gnesi [BG04]	Bertolino et al. developed Product Line Use case Test Optimization (PLUTO), a method of creating tests from the use case descriptions of a software product line. Variation points in a use case description are tagged to create a Product Line Use Case (PLUC) description. The tags in a PLUC identify alternative, optional and parametric variation points. They then applied category partition testing to product line use cases.

Table 2.4: Related Work for Software Product Line Testing 1/2

Nebut et al. [NFTJ03]	Nebut et al.'s technique created customizable use case contracts for a software product line, customized these contracts for an application derived from a software product line and then applied predicate-based testing coverage criteria on these contracts.
Kamsties et al. [KPRR03]	Kamsties et al. created activity diagrams from software product line use cases and then applied parameterization, fragmentation and segmentation techniques to these activity diagrams in order to create reusable test cases.
Hartmann et al. [HVFR05]	Hartmann et al. developed a tool that converts activity diagrams to category partition tests for a system, and then extended that tool for a software product line. A test engineer maps product configurations to nodes and transitions in the activity diagrams. Selecting a product configuration selects and enables the nodes and transitions in the activity diagrams that correspond to that product configuration.
Geppert et al. [GLRW04]	Geppert et al. investigated the problem of test reuse in a software product line. System tests were parameterized to make them reusable and a decision tree was used to guide the test selection and customization for an application of the software product line.

Table 2.5: Related Work for Software Product Line Testing 2/2

2.2.6 State-based Software Product Line Testing

Table 2.6 represents related work in state-based Software Product Line Testing.

Offutt and Abdurazik [OA99]	UML state machines are used by Offutt and Abdurazik to derive test cases automatically.
El-Fakih et al. [EFYvB02]	They consider testing during product life cycle. They reduce the test effort by testing only the modified elements of a new product version.
Weissleder et al. [WSS08]	They propose the reuse of test models for automatic model-based test generation. They define an approach to reuse state machines for context classes from a class hierarchy. This state machine can also be used to describe the behaviour of this class' subclasses. They focus on UML state machines, OCL constraints, and inheritance relationships. The approach allows to test all products of a product line based on one behavioural test model. Test cases are generated automatically from UML models with special focus on inheritance as one part of object-orientation. The automation of the test case creation reduces the effort for repeated test creation. In this approach, the differences between the product variants can be expressed by pre-/postconditions or attribute values of context classes.
Luna and Gonzalez [LG08]	They argue that the behavior of product lines can be specified, by extending UML State Charts by introducing variability in their main components. Their contribution is the proposal of a rule-based approach that defines a transformation strategy from extended State Charts to concrete UML State Charts. This is accomplished via the use of feature models in order to describe the common and variant components in such a way that, starting from different feature configurations and applying the rule-based method, concrete state machines corresponding to different products of a line can be obtained.

Table 2.6: State-based Software Product Line Testing

2.2.7 Testing Strategies for Software Product Lines

The following table 2.12 represents the testing strategies available for software product line. Those testing strategies should consider the product line variability and the differentiation

Technical University of Ilmenau

between the two development processes, i.e. domain and application engineering.[PBvdL05] As the first two strategies, BFS and PAS, have obvious shortcomings, they are not recommended. The two remaining strategies, namely the SAS and CRS are reasonable. [PBvdL05] recommends to combine the two strategies to keep the strong points in both of them.

Testing Strategies for Software Product Lines

Brute Force Strategy (BFS)	Pure Application Strategy (PAS)	Sample Application Strategy (SAS)	Commonality and Reuse Strategy (CRS)
It performs all test activities at all level and for all possible application in the domain test. This strategy performs • component test, • integration test and • system test → for all possible configurations of variability in a SPL. No application test is required during the application engineering.	It performs testing only for a concrete product in the application engineering. No test is performed in the domain engineering. This testing strategy is similar to the test in single-product engineering. The defects found in the application engineering test may be resulted in the domain artifacts and in a unique application artifact.	It uses one or several sample application to test the domain artifacts. Each application is still systematically tested. The strategy avoids the deficiency of the before mentioned two strategies. It ensures a sufficient quality of domain artifacts by building representative applications and testing the common parts and selected variants as early as possible.	This strategy divides the product line testing into two parts: domain test and application test. Domain test aims → at testing common parts and preparing test artifacts for variable parts. Application test aims → at reusing the test artifacts for common parts and reusing the predefined, variable domain test artifacts to test specific applications.
(+) Early validation is fulfilled and no application test is required. (-)The strategy is not usable in practice, because of the huge test space. (-) No variability consideration in the test artifacts. (-) increasing time for the large amount of test artifacts to be created.	(+) The test engineer neither has to deal with absent variants nor with variability. (-)High overhead, because the test artifacts are developed all over again for each application, which has no advantage over the single-product engineering testing. (-)Lack of early validation since nothing is tested until the first application is built.	(+) Early validation, as the common parts and even some typical variants can be tested during domain engineering. (+)Variability does not occur in the documents the test engineer receives for a sample application. (-)High overhead because one or more applications have to be realized to enable testing, which is worth doing, because this application realization proves that applications can be derived from the platform.	(+)The chief advantage of the strategy is to systematically reuse the testing artifacts. (+)No application is required. (+)Variability is included in the test artifacts. (+)Test cases that affect only commonalities can be executed during domain engineering. (-)Test cases that affect variability can be executed only after the variability has been bound in application engineering. (-)The domain test must consider how to design testing artifacts containing variability, which causes the difficulty in the domain testing.

Figure 2.12: Testing Strategies for Software Product Lines[JHQJ08]

Chapter 3

Fundamentals

"Goals are not only absolutely necessary to motivate us. They are essential to really keep us alive." Robert H. Schuller

3.1 Quality Assurance and Testing

3.1.1 Introduction

Software testing is one of the most important phases in software engineering, and it plays an essential role in software quality assurance. Therefore, testing and quality assurance of embedded product lines, which is the main focus of this thesis, become extremely important to the success of embedded product line development, because a single defect may affect many components in the product line.[GTW03]

There are several different terms that need to be clarified (table 3.1) before explaining what is meant by testing and quality assurance.

Term	Meaning
Mistake	A human action that produces an incorrect result.
Fault	An incorrect step, process, or data definition in a computer program. The outgrowth of the mistake. (Potentially leads to a failure.)
Failure	An incorrect result. The result (manifestation) of the fault (e.g., a crash).
Error	The amount by which the result is incorrect.

Table 3.1: Different terms for errors[Kit95]

3.1.2 Computer System Failures caused by Software Bugs

- Email services of a major smartphone system were interrupted or unavailable for nine hours in December 2009, the second service interruption within a week, according to news reports. The problems were believed to be due to bugs in new versions of the email system software.

- A news report in January 2009 indicated that a major IT and management consulting company was still battling years of problems in implementing its own internal accounting systems, including a 2005 implementation that reportedly "was attempted without adequate testing".

- Software system problems at a large health insurance company in August 2008 were the cause of a privacy breach of personal health information for several hundred thousand customers, according to news reports. It was claimed that the problem was due to software that 'was not comprehensively tested'.

- Software problems in the automated baggage sorting system of a major airport in February 2008 prevented thousands of passengers from checking baggage for their flights. It was reported that the breakdown occurred during a software upgrade, despite pre-testing of the software. The system continued to have problems in subsequent months.

- In November of 2007 a regional government reportedly brought a multi-million dollar lawsuit against a software services vendor, claiming that the vendor 'minimized quality' in delivering software for a large criminal justice information system and the system did not meet requirements. The vendor also sued its subcontractor on the project.

- A software problem contributed to a rail car fire in a major underground metro system in April of 2007 according to newspaper accounts. The software reportedly failed to perform as expected in detecting and preventing excess power usage in equipment on new passenger rail cars, resulting in overheating and fire in the rail car, and evacuation and shutdown of part of the system.

- Tens of thousands of medical devices were recalled in March of 2007 to correct a software bug. According to news reports, the software would not reliably indicate when available power to the device was too low.

- A September 2006 news report indicated problems with software utilized in a state government's primary election, resulting in periodic unexpected rebooting of voter checkin machines, which were separate from the electronic voting machines, and resulted in confusion and delays at voting sites. The problem was reportedly due to insufficient testing.

- In early 2006 problems in a government's financial monitoring software resulted in incorrect election candidate financial reports being made available to the public. The government's election finance reporting web site had to be shut down until the software was repaired.

- Trading on a major Asian stock exchange was brought to a halt in November of 2005, reportedly due to an error in a system software upgrade. The problem was rectified and trading resumed later the same day.

- In July 2004 newspapers reported that a new government welfare management system in Canada costing several hundred million dollars was unable to handle a simple benefits rate increase after being put into live operation. Reportedly the original contract allowed for only 6 weeks of acceptance testing and the system was never tested for its ability to handle a rate increase.

- A bug in site management software utilized by companies with a significant percentage of worldwide web traffic was reported in May of 2004. The bug resulted in performance problems for many of the sites simultaneously and required disabling of the software until the bug was fixed.

- News stories in the fall of 2003 stated that a manufacturing company recalled all their transportation products in order to fix a software problem causing instability in certain circumstances. The company found and reported the bug itself and initiated the recall procedure in which a software upgrade fixed the problems.

- In March of 2002 it was reported that software bugs in Britain's national tax system resulted in more than 100,000 erroneous tax overcharges. The problem was partly attributed to the difficulty of testing the integration of multiple systems.

- A review board concluded that the NASA Mars Polar Lander failed in December 1999 due to software problems that caused improper functioning of retro rockets utilized by the Lander as it entered the Martian atmosphere.

- In early 1999 a major computer game company recalled all copies of a popular new product due to software problems. The company made a public apology for releasing a product before it was ready.

- In April of 1998 a major U.S. data communications network failed for 24 hours, crippling a large part of some U.S. credit card transaction authorization systems as well as other large U.S. bank, retail, and government data systems. The cause was eventually traced to a software bug.

- January 1998 news reports told of software problems at a major U.S. telecommunications company that resulted in no charges for long distance calls for a month for 400,000 customers. The problem went undetected until customers called up with questions about their bills.

- A retail store chain filed suit in August of 1997 against a transaction processing system vendor (not a credit card company) due to the software's inability to handle credit cards with year 2000 expiration dates.

- On June 4 1996 the first flight of the European Space Agency's new Ariane 5 rocket failed shortly after launching, resulting in an estimated uninsured loss of a half billion dollars. It was reportedly due to the lack of exception handling of a floating-point error in a conversion from a 64-bit integer to a 16-bit signed integer.[Cen07]

3.1.3 Reasons for Bugs in Software

- Miscommunication or no communication - as to specifics of what an application should or shouldn't do (the application's requirements).

- Software complexity - the complexity of current software applications can be difficult to comprehend for anyone with no experience in modern-day software development.

- Programming errors - programmers, like anyone else, can make mistakes.

- Changing requirements.

- Time pressures - scheduling of software projects is difficult at best, often requiring a lot of guesswork. When deadlines loom and the crunch comes, mistakes are made.[Cen07]

3.1.4 Different Definitions for Testing

In the literature many definitions [Kit95] for testing are found:

Edward Kit in his book "Software Testing in the Real World" [Kit95] finds that definition no. 11 in (table 3.2) is the best definition.

The present author chose the following definition for testing.
Testing [Lim09] Definition:

> "Testing involves operation of a system or application under controlled conditions and evaluating the results. The controlled conditions should include both normal and abnormal conditions. Testing should intentionally attempt to make things go wrong to determine if things happen when they shouldn't or things don't happen when they should. It is oriented to 'detection'."

On the other hand, Software Quality Assurance[Lim09] is defined as follows:

> "Software QA involves the entire software development process - monitoring and improving the process, making sure that any agreed-upon standards and

(1)	Establishing confidence that a program does what it is supposed to do (Hetzel,1973).
(2)	The process of executing a program or system with the intent of finding errors (Myers, 1979).
(3)	Detecting specification errors and deviations from the specifications.
(4)	An activity aimed at evaluating an attribute or capability of a program or system (Hetzel, 1983).
(5)	The measurement of software quality (Hetzel, 1983).
(6)	The process of evaluating a program or system.
(7)	Verifying that a system satisfies its specified requirements or identifying differences between expected and actual results.
(8)	Confirming that a program performs its intended functions correctly.
(9)	The process of operating a system or component under specified conditions, observing or recording the results, and making an evaluation of some aspect of the system or component (IEEE/ANSI, 1990 (Std 610.12-1990]).
(10)	The process of analysing a software item to detect the difference between existing and required conditions (that is, bugs) and to evaluate the features of the software items (IEEE/ANSI, 1983 (Std 829-1983]).
(11)	The purpose of testing is to discover errors. Testing is the process of trying to discover every conceivable fault or weakness in a work product.

Table 3.2: Historical definitions of testing[Kit95]

procedures are followed, and ensuring that problems are found and dealt with. It is oriented to 'prevention'."

Software testing is supposed to be concerned, after finding errors, with assuring the quality of the system in order to fulfill the system requirements and satisfy the customers. In other words, software testing is more than just error detection; testing software is operating the software under controlled conditions, (1)to verify that it behaves as specified; (2) to detect errors, and (3) to validate that what has been specified is what the user actually wanted.[Tri10]

3.1.5 Difference between Quality Assurance, Quality Control and Testing

Many people and organizations are confused about the difference between quality assurance (QA), quality control (QC), and testing. Though they are closely related in meaning, but they have different concepts.

Based on ANSI/IEEE standards, they are defined as follows[Gee10]:

- **Testing**: The process of executing a system with the intent of finding defects including test planning prior to the execution of the test cases.

- **Quality Control**: A set of activities designed to evaluate a developed working product.

- **Quality Assurance**: A set of activities designed to ensure that the development and/or maintenance process is adequate to ensure a system will meet its objectives.

QA activities ensure that the process is defined and appropriate. Methodology and standards development are examples of QA activities. A QA review would focus on the process elements of a project (e.g., are requirements being defined at the proper level of detail?). QC activities focus on finding defects in specific deliverables (e.g., are the defined requirements the right requirements?). Testing is one example of a QC activity, but there are others such as inspections. The difference is that QA is process oriented and QC is product oriented. Testing therefore is product oriented and thus falls in the QC domain. Testing for quality is not assuring quality, it is controlling it. Quality Assurance ensures that the right things are done the right way. Quality Control ensures that the results meet the users expectations.

Technical University of Ilmenau

Quality Assurance	Testing
QA is a continuous process in which we monitor and perform steps in order to improve.	Testing is done under controlled conditions in order to find defects.
The role of quality assurance is a superset of testing.	It is one example of Quality Control activity.
QUALITY ASSURANCE measures the quality of processes used to create a quality product.	QUALITY CONTROL measures the quality of a product.
The goal of QA is to prevent the errors in the program.	The goal of testing is to find the errors.
It is **PREVENTION** oriented.	It is **DETECTION** oriented.

Table 3.3: Quality Assurance versus Testing[Lew04][Cen07]

In their Systematic Software Testing book [CJ02], Craig and Jaskiel explained, "Testing is a concurrent life cycle process of engineering, using, and maintaining test ware in order to measure and improve the quality of the software being tested."

In this definition, there is no direct mention of finding defects, although it is certainly still a valid goal of testing. This definition also includes not only measuring, but also improving the quality of the software. This is known as preventive testing. It uses the philosophy that testing can actually improve the quality of the software being tested if it occurs early enough in the life cycle. Specially, preventive testing requires the creation of test cases to validate the requirements before the code is written. The process of writing test cases to test a requirement (before the design or code is completed) can identify flaws in the requirements specification. Problems in the requirements can be very costly to fix, especially if they are not discovered until after the code is written, because this may necessitate the rewriting of the code, design and/or requirements. By following this approach, the main benefits are software documentation, cost reduction, time investment and early detection of errors.[CJ02]

Using the Rational Unified Process (RUP) in an iterative incremental way would support the preventive testing discussed in this paper. In other words, testing should be performed from the beginning of the software development life cycle in an iterative incremental manner.

In his technical report[McG01] on testing software product line, McGregor described that we should embed the test cases from the beginning of the life cycle and try to manage their reuse in order to avoid testing from scratch with each new software development. Testing in itself cannot ensure the quality of software. The testing team cannot improve quality; they can only measure it. All that testing can do is to provide a certain level of assurance (confidence) in the software. On its own, the only thing that testing proves is that under specific controlled conditions the software functions as expected by the test cases executed.[Tri10]

3.1.6 Debugging and Testing

Debugging and testing are different. Testing can show failures that are caused by defects. Debugging is the development activity that identifies the cause of a defect, repairs the code and checks that the defect has been fixed correctly. Subsequent confirmation testing by a tester ensures that the fix does indeed resolve the failure. The responsibility for each activity is very different, i.e. testers test and developers debug.[IC08]

Debugging	Testing
It is a process of finding and removing errors	It is a demonstration of error or apparent correctness
It is concerned with locating and repairing these errors	It is concerned with establishing the existence of defects in a program
It starts from possibly unknown initial conditions, and the end can not be predicted, except statistically	It starts with known conditions, uses predefined procedures, and has predictable outcomes
Its procedures and duration can not be constrained	It should be designed and scheduled beforehand
It is the programmer's justification	It proves programmer's failure
It must be done by an insider	It can be done by an outsider
It can be done only with detailed design knowledge	It can be designed and accomplished without detailed design knowledge

Table 3.4: Debugging vs. Testing[Bei84]

3.1.7 How Testing should be?

Testing Should be **repeatable, systematic** and **documented**[Cen07].

- **Repeatable** means:
  if an error is found, the test should be repeated to show others; if an error is corrected, the test should be repeated to ensure successful fix.

- **Systematic** means:
  random testing is not enough; select test sets that cover the range of behaviors of the program and select test sets that are representative of real uses.

- **Documented** means:
  keep track of what tests were performed, and what the results were

3.1.8 The Test Process

A common perception of testing is that it only consists of running tests, i.e. executing the software. This is part of testing, but not all of the testing activities. The fundamental test process consists of the following main activities:

- Planning and control;
- Analysis and design;
- Implementation and execution;
- Evaluating exit criteria and reporting;
- Test closure activities.

Although logically sequential, the activities in the process may overlap or take place concurrently.[IC08]

3.1.9 Purpose of Testing

The purpose of testing is verification, validation and error detection in order to find problems and the purpose of finding those problems, is to get them fixed.

By understanding the root causes of defects found in other projects, processes can be improved, which in turn should prevent those defects from reoccurring and entails the improvement of future systems quality.

Effective testing before production deployment achieves three major benefits[IC08]:

1. Discovering defects before an application is deployed allows to fix them before they impact business operations. This reduces business disruptions from software failure or errors and reduces the cost of fixing the defects.

2. Users can estimate the extent of remaining, undiscovered defects in software and use such estimates to decide when the software meets reliability criteria for production deployment.

3. Test results help users identify strengths and deficiencies in the development processes and make process improvements that improve delivered software.

3.1.10 Testing Principles

A number of testing principles have been suggested over the past 40 years and offer common guidelines for all testing. These should be the fundamentals for a positive testing organization approach. [GvVEB06]

- **Principle 1** - Testing shows only presence of defects.
  Testing can show that defects are present, but cannot prove that there are no defects. Testing reduces the probability of undiscovered defects remaining in the software but, even if no defects are found, it is not a proof of correctness.

- **Principle 2** - Exhaustive testing is impossible.
  Testing everything (all combinations of inputs and preconditions) is not feasible except for trivial cases. Instead of exhaustive testing, risks and priorities are used to focus testing efforts.

- **Principle 3** - Early testing.
  Testing activities should start as early as possible in the software or system development life cycle, and should be focused on defined objectives.

- **Principle 4** - Defect clustering.
  A small number of modules contain most of the defects discovered during prerelease testing, or show the most operational failures.

- **Principle 5** - Pesticide paradox.
  If the same tests are repeated over and over again, eventually the same set of test cases will no longer find any new bugs. To overcome this "pesticide paradox", the test cases need to be regularly reviewed and revised, and new and different tests need to be written to exercise different parts of the software or system to potentially find more defects.

- **Principle 6** - Testing is context dependent.

  Testing is variably done in different contexts. For example, safety-critical software is tested differently from an e-commerce site.

- **Principle 7** - Absence-of-errors fallacy.

  Finding and fixing defects does not help if the system built is unusable and does not fulfill the users' needs and expectations.

3.1.11 Software Testing Types

This part lists different types of testing and the main ones are depicted in figure 3.1.

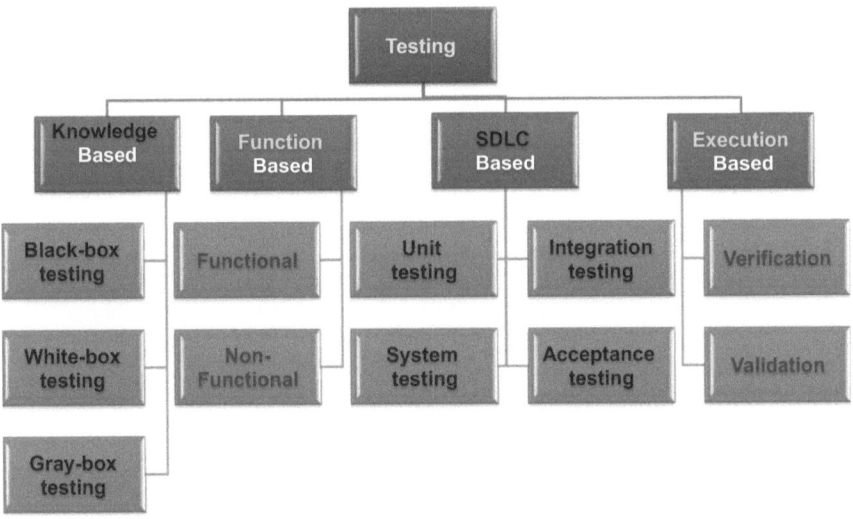

Figure 3.1: Different Types of Testing

- **ACCEPTANCE TESTING**

Testing to verify that a product meets customer specified requirements. A customer usually does this type of testing on a product that is developed externally.

- **BLACK-BOX TESTING**

  Testing without knowledge of the internal workings of the item being tested. Tests are usually functional.

- **COMPATIBILITY TESTING**

  Testing to ensure compatibility of an application or Web site with different browsers, OSs, and hardware platforms. Compatibility testing can be performed manually or can be driven by an automated functional or regression test suite.

- **CONFORMANCE TESTING**

  Verifying implementation conformance to industry standards. Producing tests for the behavior of an implementation to be sure it provides the portability, interoperability, and/or compatibility a standard defines.

- **FUNCTIONAL TESTING**

  Validating that an application or Web site conforms to its specifications and correctly performs all its required functions. This entails a series of tests which perform a feature by feature validation of behavior, using a wide range of normal and erroneous input data. This can involve testing of the product's user interface, APIs, database management, security, installation, networking, etcF testing can be performed on an automated or manual basis using black box or white box methodologies.

- **INTEGRATION TESTING**

  Testing in which modules are combined and tested as a group. Modules are typically code modules, individual applications, client and server applications on a network, etc. Integration Testing follows unit testing and precedes system testing.

- **LOAD TESTING**

  Load testing is a generic term covering Performance Testing and Stress Testing.

- **PERFORMANCE TESTING**

  Performance testing can be applied to understand your application or WWW site's scalability, or to benchmark the performance in an environment of third party products such as servers and middleware for potential purchase. This sort of testing is particularly useful to identify performance bottlenecks in high use applications. Performance testing generally involves an automated test suite as this allows easy simulation of a variety of normal, peak, and exceptional load conditions.

- **REGRESSION TESTING**

  Similar in scope to a functional test, a regression test allows a consistent, repeatable validation of each new release of a product or Web site. Such testing ensures that reported product defects have been corrected for each new release and that no new quality problems were introduced in the maintenance process. Though regression testing can be performed manually, an automated test suite is often used to reduce the time and resources needed to perform the required testing.

- **SMOKE TESTING**

  A quick-and-dirty test to ensure that the major functions of a piece of software work without bothering with finer details. Originated in the hardware testing practice of turning on a new piece of hardware for the first time and considering it a success if it does not catch on fire.

- **STRESS TESTING**

  Testing conducted to evaluate a system or component at or beyond the limits of its specified requirements to determine how and under what load it fails. A graceful degradation under load leading to non-catastrophic failure is the desired result. Stress Testing is often performed using the same process as Performance Testing but employing a very high level of simulated load.

- **SYSTEM TESTING**

  Testing conducted on a complete, integrated system to evaluate the system's compliance with its specified requirements. System testing falls within the scope of black box testing, and as such, should require no knowledge of the inner design of the code or logic.

- **UNIT TESTING**

Functional and reliability testing in an Engineering environment. Producing tests for the behavior of components of a product to ensure their correct behavior prior to system integration.

- **WHITE BOX TESTING**
  Testing based on an analysis of internal workings and structure of a piece of software. It includes techniques such as Branch Testing and Path Testing. It is also known as Structural Testing and Glass Box Testing. [Apt10]

3.1.12 Comparison between Black-Box Testing & White-Box Testing

Broad Comparison among the two prime testing techniques i.e. Black Box Testing & White Box Testing are as under Table 3.5

Black Box Testing	White Box Testing
Functional Testing	Glass Box Testing or Structural Testing
Focus on Results	Focus on Details
Called "Black Box" testing because no knowledge of the internal logic of the system is used to develop test cases	Referred to as "White Box" testing because knowledge of the internal logic of the system is used to develop hypothetical test cases
Uses validation techniques	Uses verification techniques
Tests are based on requirements and functionality	Tests are based on coverage of code statements, branches, paths, conditions
Simulates actual system usage	Allows for testing structures logic
Pros: Easy to Use, Rapid	Pros: Stable and Thorough
Cons: Vulnerability of code changes	Cons: Complexity

Table 3.5: Black-Box Testing & White-Box Testing

The targeted test here is a requirements model based system test that takes variability into consideration. System testing falls within the scope of black box testing, and as such, should require no knowledge of the inner logic or design of the code.

3.2 Unified Modeling Language(UML)

3.2.1 Building Models

Models are built to develop software that satisfies their intended purpose and can adapt to the changing needs of business and technology. Modeling is the central part of all the activities that lead up to the deployment of good software. Development of the software engineering discipline is similar to building construction industry. Like other engineering disciplines, software engineers build models of the software system before carrying out the actual implementation. Modeling is a very important activity in software development since the software engineer usually spends a lot of time developing models with different levels of abstraction before the software system is finally designed and implemented. Models are an effective communication tool, especially in situations where detailed information is not required.[Tsa05] Different stakeholders invariably need information about different aspects of the physical system. Therefore, different models should be created for them. A model contains different views (one or more), with each view representing a specific aspect of the system. [Tsa05] Models are built to visualize and control the system's architecture. 1) To better understand the system so that it is easily simplified and reused. 2) To manage risks. 3) A model is a simplification of reality. 4) A model provides the blueprints of a system. 5) Models are usually built for complex systems because we cannot comprehend such a system in its entirety. 6) No single model is sufficient. 7) Every nontrivial system is best approached through a small number of nearly independent models (models that can be built and studied separately but are still interrelated).

3.2.2 Visual Modeling

The human brain is capable of handling and processing only a limited amount of information at any time. Models can help reduce complexity by creating an abstract hierarchical representation of the real world system. Creating models through abstraction using some standard graphical notations is a fundamental technique used to perceive world. In the object oriented approach, the visual modeling language used to specify models of a system for software development is Unified Modeling Language (UML). [Tsa05]

3.2.3 UML

UML started as an effort by Booch and Rumbaugh in 1994 not only to create a common notation, but also to combine their two methods - the Booch and OMT methods. Thus, the first public draft of what is known today as the UML was presented as the Unified Method. They were soon joined at Rational Corporation by Ivar Jacobson, the creator of the Objectory method, and as a group came to be known as the three amigos. It was at this point that they decided to reduce the scope of their effort, and focus on a common diagramming notation - the UML. [Lar04] UML is accepted by the Object Management Group (OMG) as the standard for modeling object oriented programs. It is a relatively open standard, controlled by the OMG. [Fow03]. The simple and essential value of the UML Diagrams help us see or explore more of the big picture and relationships between analysis or software elements, while allowing us to ignore or hide uninteresting details. ([Lar04].

3.2.4 UML Definition

Fowler made the following simplified definition for UML:

> "The Unified Modeling Language (UML) is a family of graphical notations, backed by single meta-model, that help in describing and designing software systems, particularly software systems built using the object-oriented (OO) style." [Fow03]

The following definition was given by the OMG:

> "The Unified Modeling Language is a visual language for specifying, constructing and documenting the artifacts of system." [OMG03a]

The current version of the standard is UML 2.2(figure 3.2). UML is technology independent and can be used with all processes throughout the software development life cycle. Good models ensure technical and architectural soundness, particularly for complex systems.

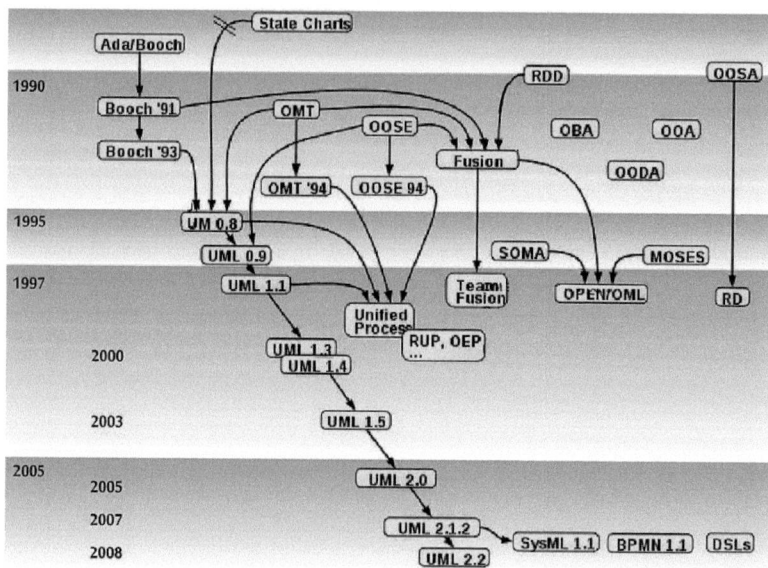

Figure 3.2: OO-historie

3.2.5 Diagrams overview

UML 2.2 has 14 types of diagrams divided into two categories (figure 3.3). Seven diagram types represent structural information, and the other seven represent general types of behavior, including four that represent different aspects of interactions. These diagrams can be categorized hierarchically as shown in the following class diagram:

3.3 Petri Nets (PNs) and Colored Petri Nets (CPNs)

3.3.1 Petri Nets (PNs)

Petri nets (figure 3.4)[vdA10] are a mathematically precise model, and so both the structure and the behavior of Petri net models can be described using mathematical concepts. The Petri net concepts are described briefly as follows. By mathematical definition, a Petri net is

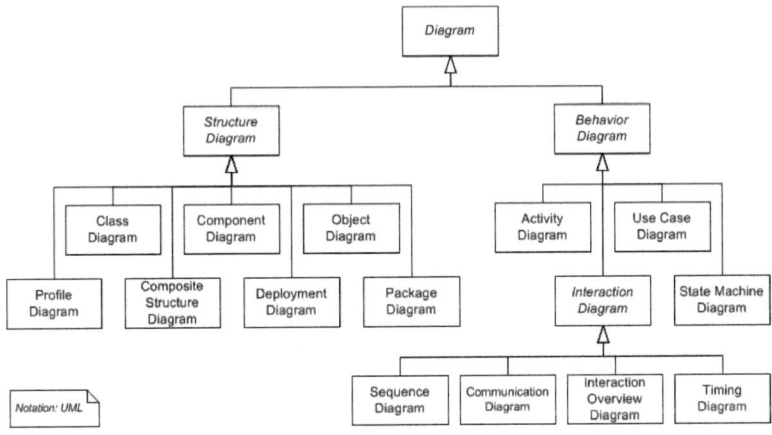

Figure 3.3: UML Diagram[OMG09]

a bipartite, directed graph consisting of a set of nodes and a set of arcs, supplemented with a distribution of tokens in places. A bipartite graph is a graph with a set of two types of nodes and no arc connecting two nodes of the same type. For (ordinary) Petri nets, we use the following three-tuple definition: $PN = (T, P, A)$, where $T = \{t_1, t_2, ..., t_n\}$, a set of nodes called transitions, $P = \{p_1, p_2, ..., p_m\}$, a set of nodes called places, $A \subseteq (T \times P) \cup (P \times T)$, a set of directed arcs. To each arc a non-negative integer multiplicity is assigned as follows $A \rightarrow N$. Note that an arc connects a transition to a place or a place to a transition. The distribution of tokens among places at certain time defines the current state of the modeled system. Transitions are enabled to fire when certain conditions are satisfied, resulting in a change of token distribution for places. With its formal representation and well-defined syntax and semantics, Petri nets can be "executed" to perform model analysis and verification. [HS06]

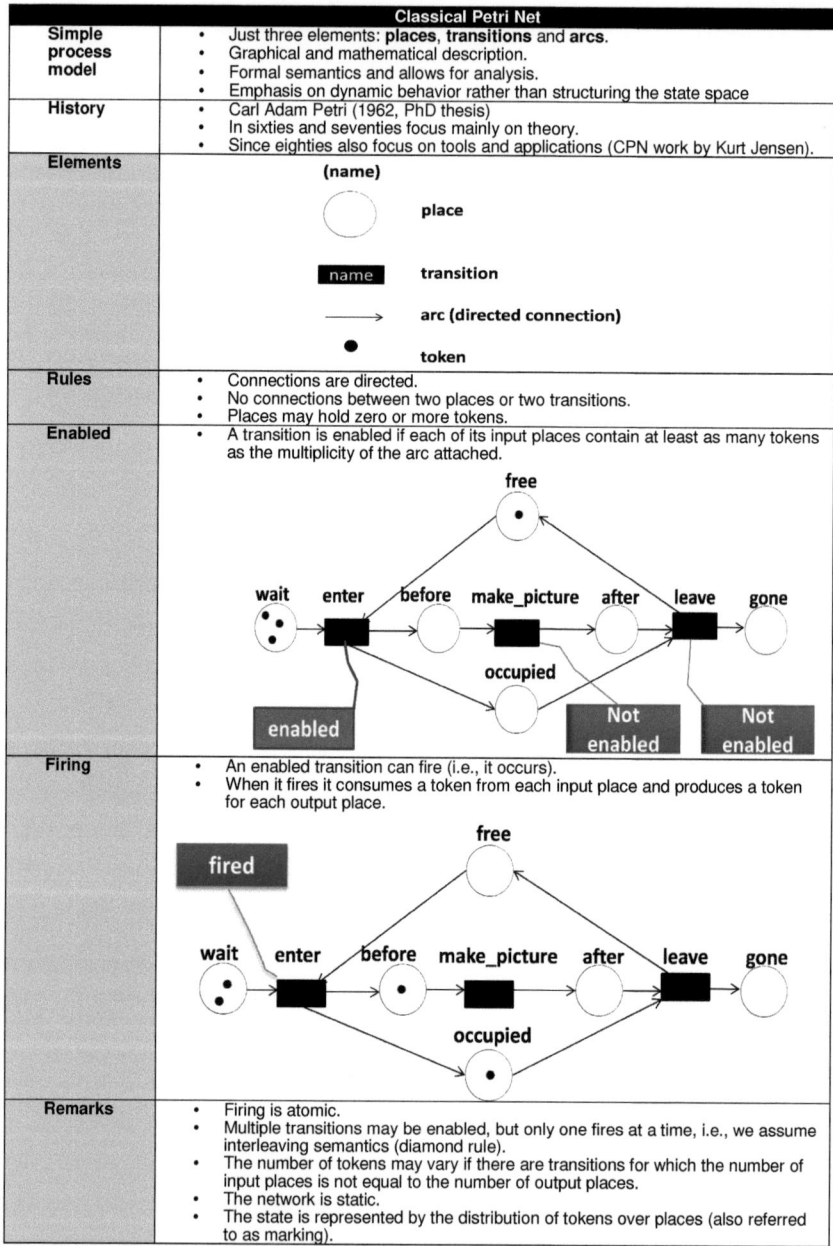

	Classical Petri Net
Simple process model	• Just three elements: **places**, **transitions** and **arcs**. • Graphical and mathematical description. • Formal semantics and allows for analysis. • Emphasis on dynamic behavior rather than structuring the state space
History	• Carl Adam Petri (1962, PhD thesis) • In sixties and seventies focus mainly on theory. • Since eighties also focus on tools and applications (CPN work by Kurt Jensen).
Elements	(name) place name transition ⟶ arc (directed connection) ● token
Rules	• Connections are directed. • No connections between two places or two transitions. • Places may hold zero or more tokens.
Enabled	• A transition is enabled if each of its input places contain at least as many tokens as the multiplicity of the arc attached.
Firing	• An enabled transition can fire (i.e., it occurs). • When it fires it consumes a token from each input place and produces a token for each output place.
Remarks	• Firing is atomic. • Multiple transitions may be enabled, but only one fires at a time, i.e., we assume interleaving semantics (diamond rule). • The number of tokens may vary if there are transitions for which the number of input places is not equal to the number of output places. • The network is static. • The state is represented by the distribution of tokens over places (also referred to as marking).

Figure 3.4: Classical Petri Net[vdA10]

3.3.2 Colored Petri Nets (CPNs)

Coloured Petri Nets have been developed from being a promising theoretical model to being a full-fledged language for the design, specification, simulation, validation and implementation of large software systems.[Jen97]

"Coloured Petri Nets (CP-nets or CPNs) is a language for the modelling and analysis of distributed systems and others systems in which concurrency, communication, resource sharing and other kinds of synchronisation plays a crucial role."[Jen07]

Typical examples of application areas are communication protocols, distributed systems, embedded systems, automated production systems, work flow analysis and VLSI chips.[Jen97]

Hence, Colored Petri nets are one type of Petri net. In colored Petri nets, tokens are differentiated by colors, which are data types. Places are typed by color sets, which specify which type of tokens can be deposited into a certain place. Arcs are associated with inscriptions, which are expressions defined with data values, variables, and functions. Arc inscriptions are used to specify the enabling condition of the associated transition as well as the tokens that are to be generated by the transition. [HS06]

Coloured Petri Nets are named as such because they allow the use of tokens that carry data values and can hence be distinguished from each other, in contrast to the tokens of low-level Petri nets, which by convention are drawn as black, "uncoloured" dots.

3.3.3 CPN-Graphical Representation

CP-nets have an intuitive, graphical representation which is appealing to human beings. A CPN model consists of a set of modules (pages) each of which contains a network of places, transitions and arcs. The modules interact with each other through a set of well-defined interfaces in a similar way to that of many modern programming languages. The graphical representation makes it easy to see the basic structure of a complex CPN model, i.e., understand how the individual processes interact with each other.[Jen97]

3.3.4 CPN-Formal Representation

CP-nets also have a formal, mathematical representation with a well-defined syntax and semantics. This representation is the foundation for the definition of the different behavioural properties and the analysis methods. Without this mathematical representation it would have been totally impossible to develop a sound and powerful CPN language. However, for the practical use of CP-nets and their tools, they managed to have an intuitive understanding of the syntax and semantics. This is analogous to programming languages which are successfully applied by users who are not familiar with the formal, mathematical definitions of the languages.[Jen97]

3.3.5 CPN and Simulation

CP-nets can be simulated interactively or automatically. In an interactive simulation, the user is in control. It is possible to see the effects of the individual steps directly on the graphical representation of the CP-net. This means that the user can investigate the different states and choose between the enabled transitions. An interactive simulation is similar to single-step debugging. It provides a way to "walk through" a CPN model, investigating different scenarios and checking whether the model works as expected. This is in contrast to many off-the-shelf simulation packages which often act as black boxes, where the user can define inputs and inspect the results, but otherwise has very little possibility to understand and validate the models on which the simulations are built. The insight and detailed knowledge of a system, which the users gain during the development and validation of a simulation model is often as important as the results that the users get from the actual simulation runs. Automatic simulations are similar to program executions. Now the purpose is to be able to execute the CPN models as fast and efficiently as possible, without detailed human interaction and inspection. However, the user still needs to interpret the simulation results. For this purpose, it is often suitable to use animated, graphical representations providing an abstract, application-specific view of the current state and activities in the system.[Jen97]

3.3.6 CPN and Verification

CP-nets also offer formal verification methods, known as state space analysis and invariant analysis. In this way, it is possible to prove, in the mathematical sense of the word, that a system has a certain set of behavioural properties. However, industrial systems are often so complex that it is impossible or at least very expensive to make a full proof of system correctness. Hence, the formal verification methods should be seen as a complement to the more informal validation by means of simulation. The use of formal verification is often restricted to the most important subsystems or the most important aspects of a complex system. [Jen07]

3.4 State Charts and Colored State Charts

3.4.1 State Charts

State Charts is a formalism designed to describe the behaviour of reactive systems, A reactive system is a mainly event-driven system, continuously reacting to external and internal stimuli. In contrast to transformational systems, that perform transformations on inputs, thus producing outputs, reactive systems engage in continuous interactions, dialogues so to say, with their environment. As a consequence, a reactive system cannot be modeled by giving its input and output alone. It is necessary to model also the timing or causality relation between input and output events. State Charts generalise Finite State Machines (FSM's), or rather Mealy machines, and arise out of a conscious attempt to free FSM's from two serious limitations: the absence of a notion of hierarchy or modularity and the ability to model concurrent behaviour in a concise way. The external and internal stimuli are called events and they cause transitions from one state to another.

States, in contrast to FSM's, can be structured as a tree. The descendants in such a tree are called substates. In State Charts, there are two types of states: the AND-type and the OR-type. Being in an AND-state means being in all of its immediate substates simultaneously. These immediate substates and their interior are called the orthogonal components of that AND-state describing concurrency. Being in an OR-state means being in exactly one of its substates.[HGdR88]

CHAPTER 3

The following figure 3.5 shows the different possible states of a State Chart, followed by figure 3.6 that shows the different possible transitions of a State Chart.

State	Graphical Representation
Normal State • Rounded rectangle, denoting a state. • Top of the rectangle contains a name of the state. • Can contain a horizontal line in the middle, below which the activities that are done in that state are indicated.	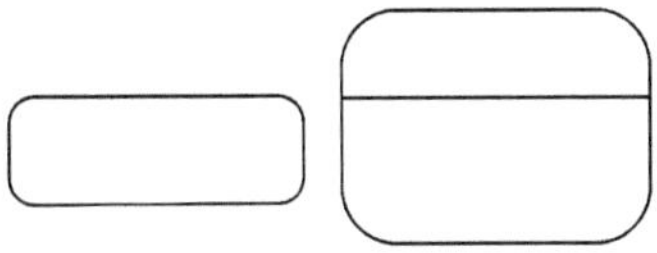
Initial state • Filled circle, pointing to the initial state. • An initial state, also called a creation state, is the one that an object is in when it is first created.	
Final State • Hollow circle containing a smaller filled circle, indicating the final state. • A final state is one in which no transitions lead out of.	

Figure 3.5: Representation of the different States of a State Chart[Mol04]

Transition	Graphical Representation
Normal	
Conditional	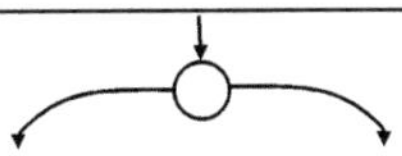
Conjunction	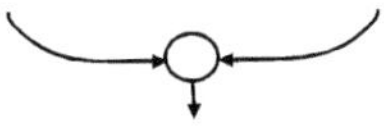
Intersection	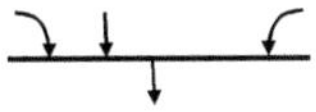
Synchronisation	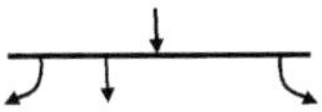

Figure 3.6: Representation of the different Transitions of a State Chart[Mol04]

Technical University of Ilmenau

The following figures 3.7, 3.8 and 3.9 shows facts about State Charts.

Facts about State Charts

What is a UML state machine diagram?

UML state machine diagrams depict the various states that an object may be in and the transitions between those states.

- A **state machine** performs **actions** in response to **explicit events**.
- A state machine is idle when it sits in a state waiting for an event to occur.
- UML state machines overcome the **main limitations** of traditional finite state machines while retaining their main benefits.
- UML State Charts introduce the new concepts of
  - **hierarchically nested states,**
  - **orthogonal regions**,
  - and **extending the notion of actions.**
- UML state machines have the characteristics of both **Mealy machines** and **Moore machines**. They support actions that depend on both the state of the system and the triggering event, as in Mealy machines, as well as entry and exit actions, which are associated with states rather than transitions, as in Moore machines.
- The term **"UML state machine"** can refer to two kinds of state machines: **behavioral state machines** and **protocol state machines**.
  - **Behavioral state machines** can be used to model the behavior of individual entities (e.g., class instances).
  - **Protocol state machines** are used to express usage protocols and can be used to specify the legal usage scenarios of classifiers, interfaces, and ports.

UML state machine diagram Synonyms:

UML state machine, known also as UML statechart → is an object-based variant of Harel statechart adapted and extended by the Unified Modeling Language. In other modeling languages, it is common for **UML state machine diagrams** to be called a **state-transition diagram** or even simply a **state diagram**.

Figure 3.7: Facts about State Charts 1/3[Amb09][Wik10]

CHAPTER 3

Hierarchy FSM will be **in** exactly one of the substates of S if S is **active** (either in A or in B or ..)	
• Current states of FSMs are also called **active states**. • States which are not composed of other states are called **basic states**. • States containing other states are called **super-states**. • For each basic state S, the super-states containing S are called **ancestor states**. • Super-states S are called **OR-super-states**, if exactly one of the sub-states of S is active whenever S is active.	
Default state Filled circle indicates sub-state entered whenever super-state is entered. Not a state by itself!	
History mechanism For input m, S enters the state it was in before S was left (can be A, B, C, D, or E). If S is entered for the first time, the default mechanism applies. History and default mechanisms can be used	

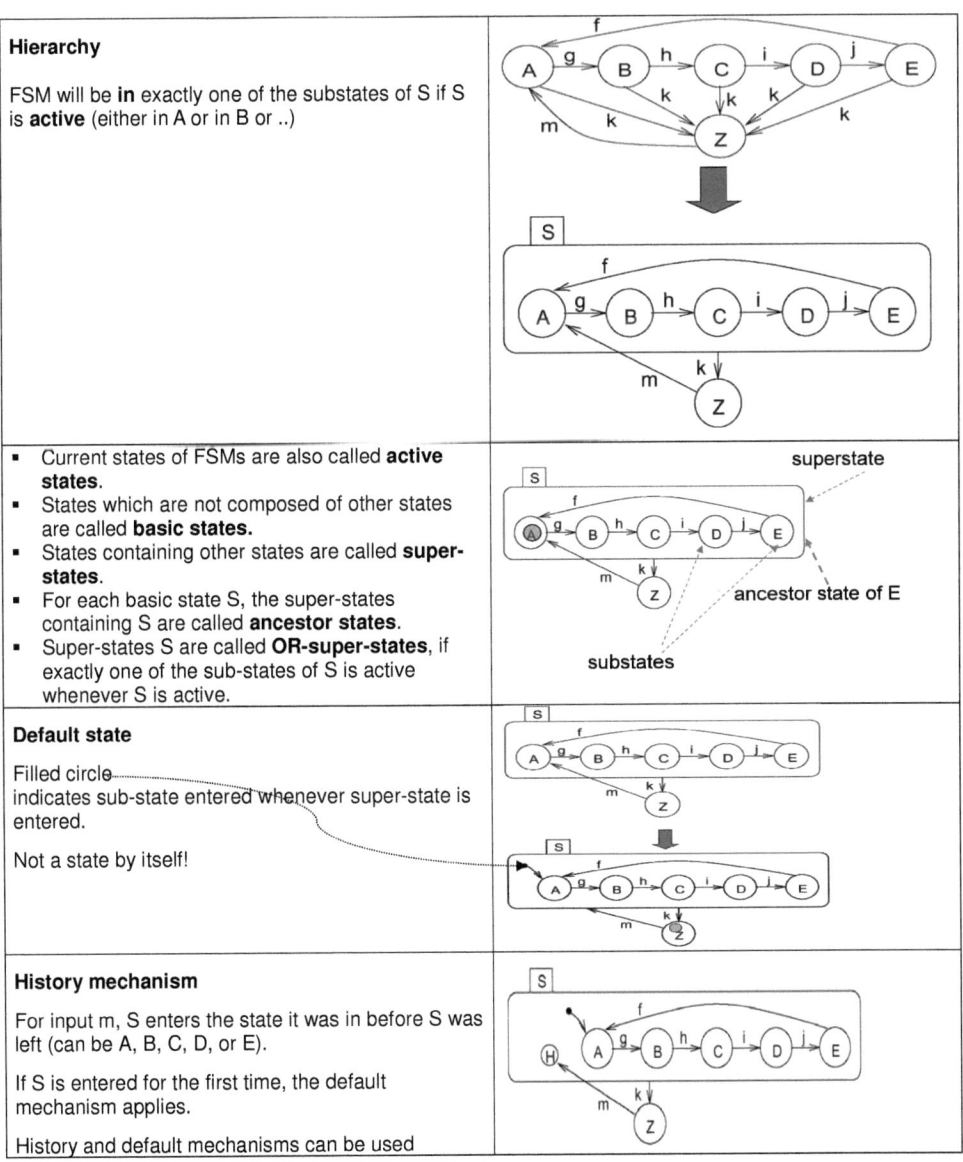

Figure 3.8: Facts about State Charts 2/3 [Mar05] [Mar09]

Types of states

In State Charts, states are either

- **Basic states**, or (States which are not composed of other states are called **basic states**.)
- **OR-super-states**, or
- **AND-super-states**.

OR-states have sub-states that are related to each other by exclusive-or. The FSM on the right side can only be in one of the sub-states of super-state Sat any time. Super states of this type are called OR-super-states.	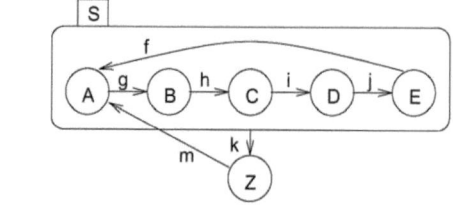
Concurrency Convenient ways of describing concurrency are required. **AND-super-states**: FSM is in all (immediate) sub-states of a super-state;	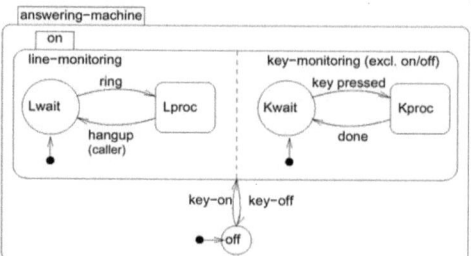
General form of edge labels The general syntax of an expression labeling a transition in a State Chart is *n[c]/a*, where ***n*** is the *event* that triggers the transition ***c*** is the *condition* that guards the transition (cannot be taken unless c is true when e occurs) ***a*** is the *action* that is carried out if and when the transition is taken.	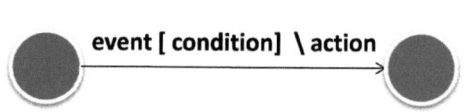

Figure 3.9: Facts about State Charts 3/3 [Mar05] [Mar09]

3.4.2 Colored State Chart(CSC)

The new approach represented in section 7.2 is called CMBT-SWPL using the CSC[FFDD02] [Fen04], where only one State Chart is depicted that captures all product line variants. One Color represents a product line variant, where features are the color variables. One Color, i.e. one product line variant, may consist of one or more features in this case color variables. (See section 7.2 on page 99 for more details).

3.5 Embedded Systems

3.5.1 Introduction to Embedded Systems

Embedded systems[Mar05] are expected to be the most important application area of information technology during the coming years. Based on this, the term post-PC era was coined. This term denotes the fact that in the future standard PCs will be less dominant kind of hardware. Processors and software will be used in much smaller systems and will in many cases even be invisible (this led to the term the disappearing computer). However, with this new trend, computers will actually not disappear; they will be rather everywhere. This new type of information technology applications has also been called ubiquitous computing, pervasive computing, and ambient intelligence. These three terms focus on only slightly different aspects of future information technology.

- **Ubiquitous Computing** focuses on the long term goal of providing "information anytime, anywhere".

- **Pervasive Computing** focuses a somewhat more on practical aspects and the exploitation of already available technology.

- **Ambient Intelligence** focuses on communication technology in future homes and smart buildings.

Embedded systems are one of the origins of these three area and they provide a major part of the necessary technology. Therefore, the embedded system is defined [Mar05] as follows:

"Embedded systems are information processing systems that are embedded into a larger product and that are normally not directly visible to the user."

Bruce Douglass [Dou04] mentions that "embedded computerized systems can be seen everywhere. There are more computers hidden in the guts of things than there are conventional desktops or laptops." Embedded systems span all aspects of modern life and there are many examples of their use. From the washing machine and microwave oven to the telephone, stereo, television, and automobile, embedded computers are everywhere. Embedded computers are even more widespread in the industry where they are used to securely and conveniently improve our productivity and quality of life.

The software for these embedded computers is more difficult to construct than the software for a desktop or laptop. Embedded systems have all the problems of desktop applications plus many more. The embedded computer is part of a lager system that provides some non-computing feature to the user. They do not have a conventional computer display or keyboard, but lie at the heart of some apparently non-computerized device. The user of these devices may never be aware of the CPU embedded within, making decisions about how and when the system should act[Dou04].

3.5.2 Embedded Systems Characteristics

The common characteristics [Dou04] [Mar05] of these embedded systems are as follows:

- Embedded systems are connected to the physical environment through sensors collecting information about that environment and actuators controlling the environment.

- Many embedded systems are safety-critical and therefore have to be dependable. Dependability encompass the following aspects of a system:
  Reliability - Maintainability - Availability - Safety - Security.

- Embedded systems have to be efficient regarding the following: energy, code size, run-time efficiency, weight and cost.

- These systems are dedicated towards a certain application. They are designed to do some specific task, rather than to be a general-purpose computer for multiple tasks.

- Most embedded systems do not use keyboards, mice and large computer monitors for their user interface.

- Many embedded systems must meet real time constraints, for reasons such as safety and usability; others may have low or no performance requirements, allowing the system hardware to be simplified to reduce costs..

- Many embedded systems are hybrid systems in the sense that they include analog and digital parts.

- Typically embedded systems are reactive systems.

- Embedded systems are not always standalone devices. Many embedded systems consist of small computerized parts within a larger device that serves a more general purpose. For example, an embedded system in an automobile provides a specific function as a subsystem of the car itself.

- The program instructions written for embedded systems are referred to as firmware, and are stored in read-only memory or Flash memory chips. They run with limited computer hardware resources: little memory, small or non-existent keyboard and/or screen.

Actually, not every embedded system will have all the above characteristics. We can define the term "embedded system" also in the following way:

"Information processing systems meeting most of the characteristics listed above are called embedded systems"

3.5.3 Reactive Embedded Systems

The term reactive [Dou04] is applied to objects that respond dynamically to incoming events of interest and whose behavior is driven by the order of arrival of those events. Such objects are usually modeled and often implemented as finite state machines. State Charts make modeling reactive objects viable. A finite state machine (FSM) specifies the events of interest to a reactive object, the set of states that object may assume, and the actions (and their order of execution) in response to incoming events in any given state. This is crucial in many systems because the allowable sequences of primitive behaviors may be restricted.

In his book *Embedded System Design*, Peter Marwedel, defined a reactive system as follows [Mar05]:

> "A reactive system is one that is in continual interaction with its environment and executes at a space determined by that environment."

Reactive systems can be thought of as being in a certain state waiting for an input. For each input, they perform some computation and generate an output and a new state. Therefore, automata are very good models of such systems. That is why State Charts have been chosen in this thesis to model the behavior of the CSC.

Chapter 4

Main Requirements of Colored Model Based Testing for Software Product Lines Method

"Nothing is Impossible, the word itself says, 'I'm Possible'!"   Audrey Hepburn

4.1 CMBT-SWPL Method's Requirements

In this section we are going to determine more precisely the main requirements of the CMBT-SWPL method and what are the steps needed to meet those requirements.

1. Reuse

    - Strategic reuse should be fulfilled for the test artifacts the same way it is fulfilled for the development artifacts.
    - The method should fulfill the reuse of Colored State Chart for systematic test case generation in the context of product lines.
    - Reusing test artifacts later in the application engineering process.
    - The components and artifacts intended for reuse must be of high quality since the components are potentially reused in many family members.

2. Early Validation

    - The main target of validation is to satisfy the intended requirements, which is achieved by answering the following question: **"Are we building the right thing?"**

For validation purposes, the CMBT-SWPL method should perform the following:

- Creating a feature model capturing all feature combinations and making sure that it represents the correct requirements.
- Create test artifacts that consider variability early in the product line development process.
    * Based on feature model, a test model using colored state charts should be created to facilitate testing process.
    * Then the test cases should be derived systematically from the test models using statistical testing.
- It is noteworthy that the defects in requirements, such as ambiguities and incompleteness, may be detected early during the development of the feature model as well as during the development of the test model, which is cheaper than correcting them in later development phases, where they can increase dramatically.
- Moreover it is possible to simulate the test model after transforming it to a Colored Petri Net. Then the error detection through simulation is more obvious and the chance to correct them early is facilitated.

3. Early Verification

    - The main target of verification is to check that the specifications are correctly met by the system and it is achieved by answering the following question: **"Are we building it right?"**

    For verification purposes, the CMBT-SWPL method should perform the following:

- Adopting certain powerful elements and concepts of Colored Petri Nets to the Colored State Charts.

- The proposed State Chart's semantics' extension will allow certain terms such as "Marking" and "Transition Firing" to be introduced to the UML state diagrams. This helps in diagnosing, tracing and finding the errors as it is performed in the Petri nets approach.

- More precisely, Product line verification will be accomplished by transforming the CSC into a CPN and thus we can benefit from the powerful analysis methods of PNs regarding e.g. how to deal with conflicts, deadlocks, and unwanted states.

4. Variability Consideration

    - The method should introduce variability early in the main components of the CSC, so that the behavior of product lines can be specified.

    - The method should preserve the variability in test cases.

5. Compact Presentation

    - The developed test model should be able to manage large numbers of feature combinations.

    - The method should provide compact presentation by representing all product line variants in one model, namely CSC.

        - To make it clear, if they were not compact then we would have to model several separate state charts, then errors are more likely to occur in each model.

        - On the other hand when the modeler will try to realize this compact presentation, he will try to avoid redundancies, ambiguities and incompleteness.

        - Thus, product line's test artifacts will be less complex, compact, expressive and help in modeling both simple and complex embedded reactive product lines.

- Effort for the CSC describing all product line features is admittedly much more than the effort for a state chart describing just one product variant. However, it requires considerably less effort than modelling and maintaining an individual State Chart for each product variant of a product line, in particular, for large product lines with dozens of features.

6. Systematic Test Case Generation

- The method should achieve systematic test case generation by following the next two principles:

    a) Model-Based Testing

    Model-based testing is an approach to systematically derive test cases in single system engineering. The CMBT-SWPL method adapts model-based testing to the product line engineering and supports the proactive reuse of test cases. In model-based testing, first a test model (i.e. CSC) is built from the requirements.

    b) Statistical Testing

    Statistical testing techniques are then applied to derive test cases.

7. Reduced development and maintenance effort and cost

    - Reducing test development time, cost and effort by reusing test artifacts such as test models and test cases.

4.2 Summary

In figure 4.1 the main requirements for the method are presented briefly.

Figure 4.1: Main Requirements of CMBT-SWPL Method

Chapter 5

Case Study : Universal Remote Control(URC)

"Go as far as you can see; when you get there, you'll be able to see farther."

J. P. Morgan.

5.1 Introduction

As an example of a system family, the Universal Remote Control, which is part of the Digital Video Project (figure 5.1) & (figure 5.2), is used to serve the practical testing and evaluation of the Colored Model Based Testing for Software Product Lines (CMBT-SWPL). This example [Die03] was conducted at the Faculty of Computer Science and Automation - Institute of Computer Engineering - Ilmenau University of Technology and it is part of the Digital Video Project(DVP)[Mef03][Str04] based on the VDR project [Gos10].

Within a group of students a digital video system was built making use of existing hardware and software components.The project goal is to develop a system family making use of adapted methods and thus, evaluating these methods. The students are taught to use the system family paradigm for the development of a software system within the context of a real-life example. In Figure (figure 5.2) a brief system overview is sketched, as a Unified Modeling Language (UML) component diagram[SRP03].

Figure 5.1: Digital Video System Example[SRP03]

5.2 Universal Remote Control

A universal remote is a remote control that can be programmed to operate different electronic devices. The Computer dictionary defines URC as follows:

> A handheld remote control that can turn on and operate any unit of equipment in a home theater system, such as an A/V receiver, cable box, TV, DVR, CD/DVD player and media hub. It uses built-in remote control codes for different models and may be able to download additional code sets from the Internet. Advanced units have a training mode that accepts signals from another remote placed head to head and assigns them to designated buttons.

Palm-Handhelds are used as a remote control via the Infrared Data Association (IrDA) Interface. It was desired to develop a concept allowing the creation of a system family which

CHAPTER 5

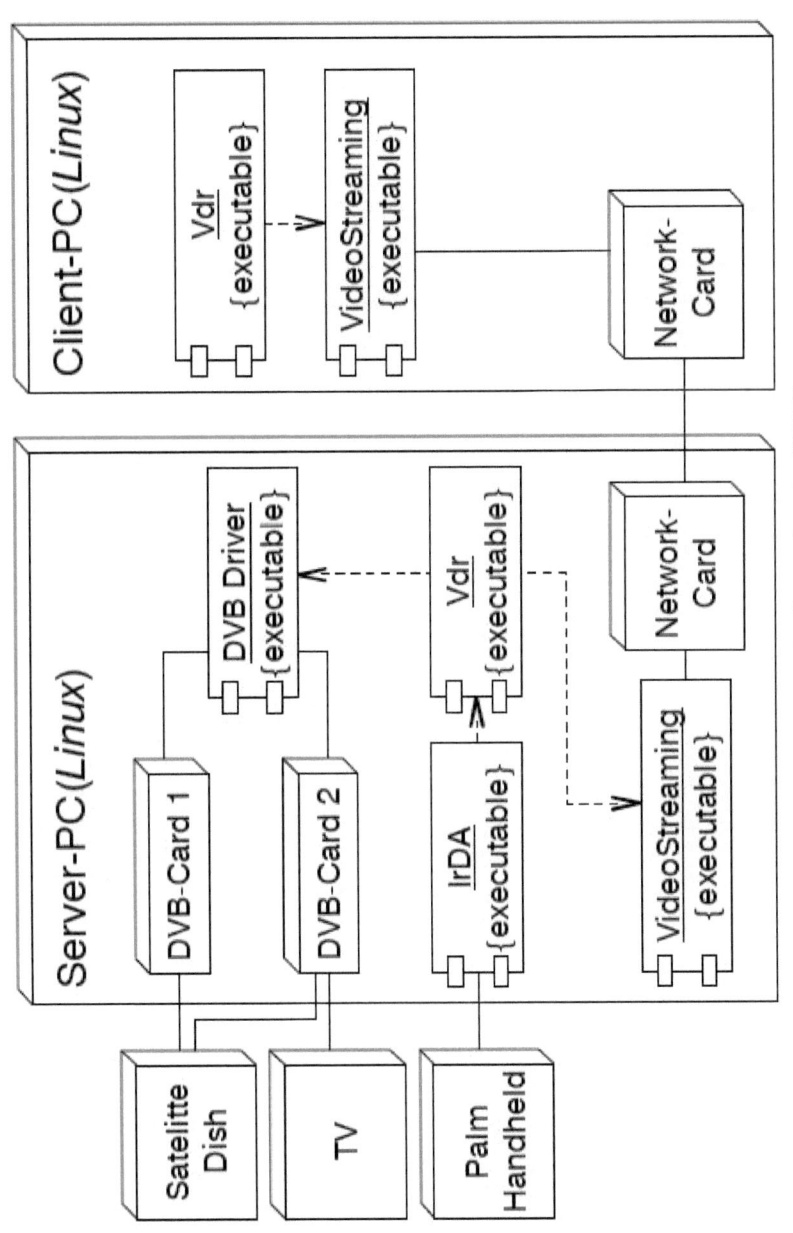

Figure 5.2: Digital Video System Overview[SRP03]

enables the combination of different features within one remote control. It was necessary to elaborate a list of the features and functions to be implemented. Furthermore, the concept should be designed in a way that different components can be combined in as desired.

A system family architecture and its integration in the current video system was developed (figure 5.2), where the interaction of this subproject with the vdr-project was considered. In [Die03] a software for Palm-Handhelds was prototypically developed to test and evaluate the elaborated concept. The target is to achieve high variability and ensure flexibility, i.e. the concept should adapt to the user needs and not vice versa.

The focus is to design a remote control that should be the central element of the operation. This universal remote control was designed as a family of systems.

Product Lines must adhere to a high level of abstraction in order to be flexible, extensible and maintainable. Many PL development methodologies have established "features" and "feature modelling" for this purpose, e.g. FODA, FORM, FeatuRSEB[SPR04]. A key technical innovation of software product-lines is the use of features to distinguish product-line members. A particular product-line member is defined by a unique combination of features. The set of all legal feature combinations defines the set of product-line members [KCH+90]. Feature models are a well accepted means for expressing requirements in a domain on an abstract level. They are applied to describe variable and common properties of products in a product line and to derive and validate configurations of software systems[Rie03].

5.3 Universal Remote Control-Feature Model

As mentioned earlier, the Palm-handheld URC is modeled using features. Figure 5.3 describes a FM for the universal remote control example. As depicted in (figure 5.3), a feature diagram has a root node called concept, referring to the complete system. Hierarchically located below the concept node are all the features of the system. Features are marked either mandatory or optional. All mandatory features are part of all systems to be generated within this family. Thus, the set of mandatory features is forming the core of the system family. At the top of the FM, the concept node **Advanced IrDA-Remote**

Control refers to the system itself. Below the concept node the **Controlling VDR** feature is modeled mandatory, since we need to control the video system in some way. At the level below the **Controlling VDR** feature, there is the mandatory **Basic Functions** feature. All features of the system are arranged hierarchically and will be marked optional or mandatory to model the core and all variable parts of the system.[SRP03] To build an application based on the system family, a selection of features has to be made. The user can choose out of all optional features of the family.

FODA [KCH+90] defines two relations between features to support the consistency of the overall model and the correctness of a choice of features in particular. With the "requires and excludes" constraints we can further limit the possible choices of features in the tree. A relation called "requires" can be established to state the need for the selection of a specific feature in case another feature should have been chosen. In our example a user might want to choose the **Title-Database** feature. This features would definitely require using the **EPG** feature.[SRP03]

A tree structure instance is an FM configuration that describes the model and that respects the semantics of their relations. That is, an FM allows one to identify common and variant features between products of a PL, while an FM configuration characterizes the functionalities of a specific product.[LG08]

The URC in [Die03] (see figure 5.3) has the following features: (1) Controlling the video recorder (2)Controlling other devices (3)Providing a user profile. All the functionalities are explained in detail in [Die03]. This thesis will focus only on how to control the video recorder. The features under focus are based on the overall feature model (see figure 5.3) in [Die03] and are reduced to the feature model of controlling the VDR represented in figure 7.4. In the reduced feature model, there are features that are mandatory such as **Basic Functions**. The **Basic Functions** feature could contain other features such as **choosing channel** feature, **controlling volume** feature or **waiting** feature. The optional features for controlling the video recorder (VDR) are **Electronic Program Guide (EPG)** and **Title-Database**. **Reminder** feature is a feature available to remind user of visual materials such as movies and is an optional sub feature of the EPG feature. **Data adjustment via telephone, programming via telephone** and **programing**

via infrared are optional sub features of EPG feature. On the other hand, the **data adjustment via infrared** is a mandatory sub-feature of EPG. **Own connection** and **connection via VDR** are two optional sub-features of **Title-Database**.

The features contained in the feature model represent aspects that concern the user. They can be divided into four categories[Str04]:

- **Functional features** expressing a behavior or interaction between the user and the system.

- **Interfaces features** expressing the integration of standards or subsystems in the product.

- **Parameters features** expressing numerical values of presentable environmental characteristics or non-functional features. In each case they have a preset value.

- **Abstract features** expressing concepts.

These characteristics are hierarchically structured in a feature model. Furthermore, the various relationships that can exist between those features are represented in this model. These relationships can be divided into several categories[Str04]:

- Features-subfeature relationships are used to reflect the hierarchy.

- Refinement· Refining involves an attempt to represent detailed sub features and express an "is-a" - or "is-part-from" relationship.

- Restrictions are expressed by "requires" and "excludes" relations.

- Recommendations or suggestions are expressed by using "hint" relationship which influences the customer selection.

Many systems are based and dependent on the flexible family architecture, which was itself based on the overall requirements for the family. Thus, requirements engineering activities have a high impact on all applications based on the family. Many of the current system family development methods are making use of feature modeling, to capture all the mandatory and optional 'parts' of the system. The feature model is a high level description

CHAPTER 5

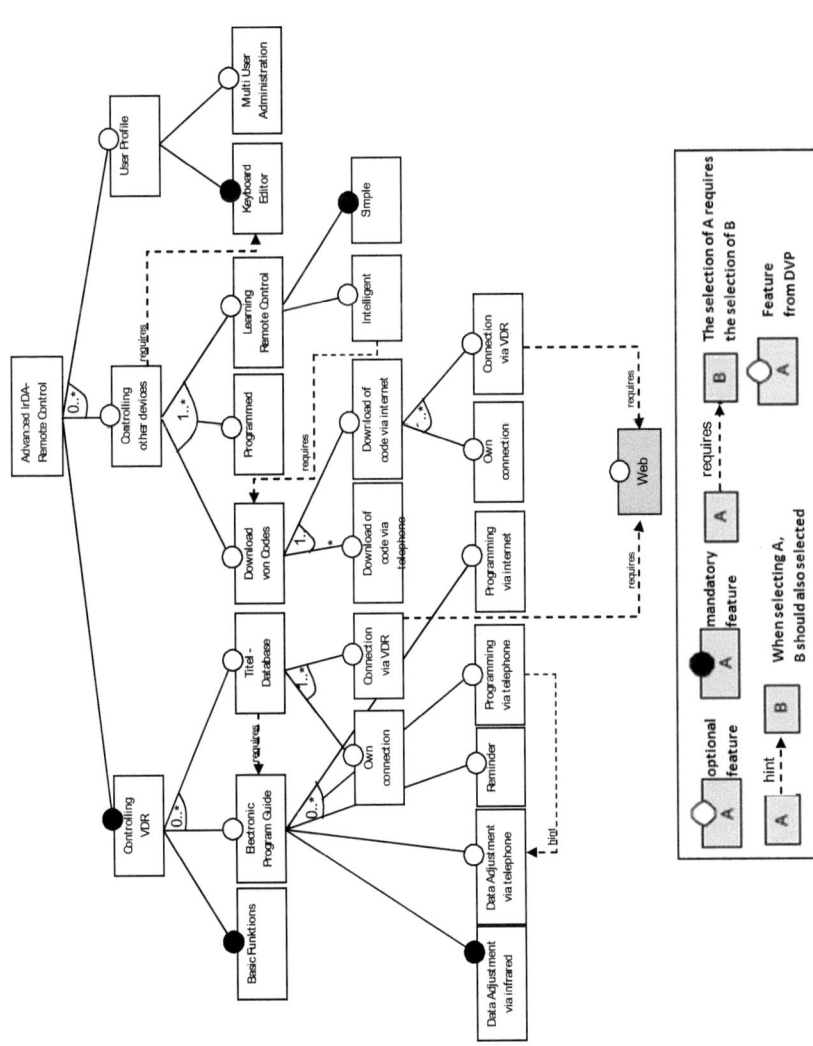

Figure 5.3: Feature Model for the Universal Remote Control [Die03]

of the system and understandable by customers.[SRP03]

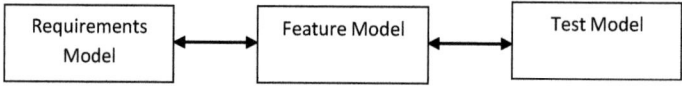

Figure 5.4: Features in context [Die03]

After completion, the feature model serves as a basic architecture for the product line. As depicted in figure 5.4, the feature model is located between the requirements model and the system design model, or more specifically in our case the test model. In the feature model, the variability and possible combinations of the individual features are taken into account. The result of this design is a generic architecture, which is generated later to a specific application. Thus, a large number of applications can be created by only changing some of the generic parameters.

In addition to the large number of applications that can be generated in a simple way, there is another advantage of system families; namely changes can be easily performed on existing architecture. Due to this modular design, it is always possible, to insert, modify or even delete individual components of the product line.[Die03]

Chapter 6

Main Aspects for Applying the Colored Model Based Testing for Software Product Lines Method

"A goal properly set is halfway reached - Abraham Lincoln"

6.1 Introduction

This chapter starts with introducing the W-model for testing software product lines. Section 6.3 & 6.4 respectively are concerned with explaining the model-based testing and the statistical testing which the CMBT-SWPL method is relied on. Section 6.5 explains the State Chart behavioral model that has been chosen from UML to capture the complex behavior of the remote control product line. Section 6.6 lists the arguments why State Charts are chosen to represent behavior.

6.2 The W-Model for Testing Software Product Lines

The traditional way of testing single systems is to test after coding is finished (for functions, components or the integrated system), i.e. when there is a running application. However, in product line testing, test development is meant to start early in the domain engineering phase and not to wait until the variability is bound and there is a running application. Therefore, testing plays an important role during software product line engineering, because the quality of the reusable domain artifacts affects all applications that are derived from these artifacts. In addition, software product line testing faces specific challenges that cannot be tackled by traditional testing techniques. Therefore, testing techniques from the development of single systems have to be adapted and/or new testing techniques have to be developed [Met06]. Thus, testing in a product line is divided into domain testing and application testing [PBvdL05].

This reusable feature-oriented model-based testing method, namely "Colored Model Based Testing for Software Product Lines lines" (CMBT-SWPL) is used to create test assets from feature models, which can then be configured to test individual applications that are members of the software product line. This method can be used to reduce the number of reusable test assets created to cover all features, and selected feature combinations of a software product line. These test assets can be automatically selected and configured during application engineering to test a given application derived from the software product line.[OG09]

McGregor [McG01] in *Testing a software product Line* states that "the testing activities are related to the construction activities in a development process. A testing activity is scheduled to immediately follow the construction activity whose output the testing activity will validate. The development process produces various types of artifacts examined by the testing process. The testing process produces test results and bug reports used by the development process to repair the artifacts. This provides an opportunity to identify defects as soon as they are injected into the artifact so that they can be removed before the faulty information is used as the basis for development in subsequent phases."[McG01]

Based on this idea [McG01][McG06], [JHQJ08] suggests a test model for SPLs. The W-model supplements domain test and application test to the dual life-cycle model of Product Line Software Engineering (PLSE), resulting in a W-form.

The W-Model suggested in [JHQJ08] seems viable compared to our approach and idea for testing the Software product line presented in Figure 2.9. In our approach, only system black box testing is stressed. Therefore, the W-Model in [JHQJ08] is merged to our reference process 2.4 and 2.5 and the resulting figure is demonstrated in figure 6.1. Three

CHAPTER 6

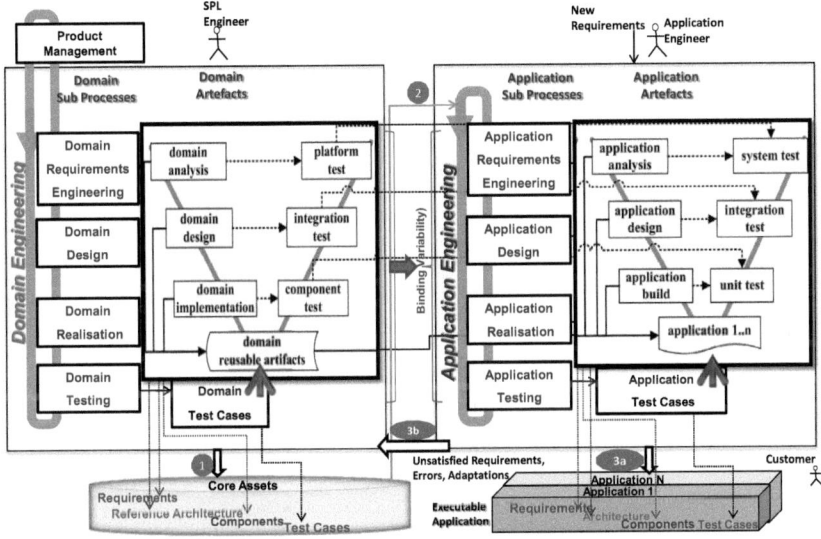

Figure 6.1: The W-Model for SPL Test

test activities at the level of component test, integration test and platform test are added to the domain engineering. They perform the tests on reusable component, SPL architecture and the common platform. Correspondingly, three test activities are inserted in the application engineering. The W-model links the closely related two kinds of software engineering activities. It ensures the quality of the common assets and the correct reuse by validating different artifacts as early as possible. The test activities in the application engineering are affected and restricted by the work in the application engineering and by the test activities of the same kind of software artifacts in the domain engineering. On the other hand, the testing results are fed back both to the domain and the application engineering to ensure that the reusable artifacts in the domain engineering are correct and adaptable to different applications. [JHQJ08]

Although the idea of this W-model is quite interesting, the missing point in this suggested test model is the variability. It is desired to create test artifacts that consider variability early in the development process, i.e. in the domain engineering in order to be reused in the application engineering.

When test artifacts are created early in the product line development process two main important principles are addressed: First, the idea of test driven development (TDD)[Bec00] is supported, which aims to design test early before coding is started; and second, embracing testing early in the development process as it is performed by the Rational Unified Process (RUP), representing evolutionary, iterative and incremental development.

Product lines would better be developed according to the RUP and not according to the waterfall-oriented requirements analysis approaches, in which there is an attempt to define so-called "complete" specifications before starting the development process. [Lar04]

6.3 Model Based Testing

The cost of finding and fixing faults in software typically rises as the development project progresses into a new phase. Faults found after the system had been delivered to the customer are much more expensive to track down and correct than if found earlier. Often testing is done when the whole system has been coded although the most expensive errors to correct are often introduced early in the life cycle. Current and future trends for software include increasingly complex requirements on interaction between systems. The increased complexity means that a system may have potentially infinite combinations of inputs and resulting outputs. It is difficult to get satisfactory coverage of such a system with hand-crafted manual or automatic test cases. Thus a method which allows the designer to automatically test the partially designed and implemented system will be of a particular value.[Bob08][BHS99]

Model-based testing (figure 6.2) is a test technique where test cases are generated from a model of the system. "More precisely, instead of manually writing hundreds of test cases (sequences of operations), the test designer writes an abstract model of the system under test, and then the model-based testing tool generates a set of test cases from that model. The overall test design time is reduced, and an added advantage is that one can generate a variety of test suites from the same model simply by using different test selection criteria."[UL06]

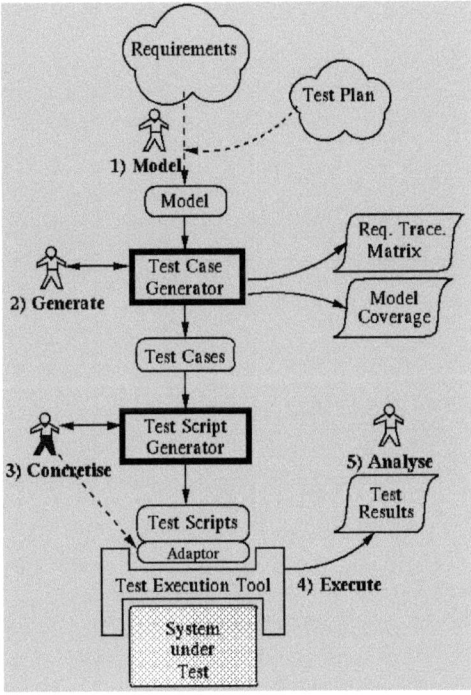

Figure 6.2: Model Based Testing

There are model-based testing tools that can automate the generation of test cases from a behavioral model, such as test oracles that can determine whether the system under test behaved correctly at the execution of the test case. Test cases generated from a model have been identified as giving a high coverage of system interaction points, given that the generation is carefully guided. It is argued that applying model-based testing in the context of product lines, starting from early development, i.e. in the domain engineering, significantly increased the number of faults found during system testing. [Bob08]

6.3.1 Model Based Testing Steps

Model-based testing is the automation of black-box test design. It usually involves four phases [Utt06]:

- Building an abstract model of the system under test.
  This is similar to the process of formally specifying the system, but the kind of specification/model needed for test generation may be a little different than that needed for other purposes, such as proving correctness, or clarifying requirements.

- Validating the model (typically via animation).
  This is done to detect gross errors in the model. This validation process is naturally incomplete, but this is less crucial in this context than in the usual refinement to code context. With model-based testing, if some errors remain in the model, they are very likely to be detected when the generated tests are run against the system under test.

- Generating abstract tests from the model.
  This step is usually automatic, but the test engineer can control various parameters to determine which parts of the system are tested, how many tests are generated, and which model coverage criteria are used etc.

- Refining those abstract tests into concrete executable tests.
  This is a classic refinement step which adds concrete details missing from the abstract model. It is usually performed automatically after the test engineer specifies a refinement function in the abstract values to some concrete values and a concrete code template for each abstract operation.

After this, the concrete tests can be executed on the system under test in order to detect failures (where the outputs of the system under test are different from those predicted by the tests). It is the redundancy of the test model and the implementation that counts. Experience shows that failures occurring when the tests are run seems to be equally due to errors in the model or errors in the implementation.

So the process of model-based testing provides useful feedback and error detection for the requirements and the model as well as the system under test.

6.3.2 Benefits of Model-Based Testing (MBT)

Model-Based Testing (MBT) can result in the following benefits[Tes10]:

- Shorter schedules, lower cost, and better quality.
- A model of user behavior.
- Enhanced communication between developers and testers.
- Early exposure of ambiguities in specification and design.
- Capability to automatically generate many non-repetitive and useful tests.
- Test harness to automatically run generated tests.
- Easy update of test suites for changed requirements.
- Capability to evaluate regression test suites.
- Capability to assess software quality.

These benefits all require an initial investment in tools and training.

6.4 Model-Based Statistical Testing

The objective of a real-life test is to detect defects concerning the operational usage of a system. The test should therefore simulate the real situation as much as possible. One method for describing the real usage of a system is called operational profiles. An operational profile is a quantitative characterization of how a system will be used. Statistical usage testing uses operational profiles to produce a statistically relevant set of test cases. Statistical usage testing pays more attention to the most frequently used operations focusing mainly on normal use of the system. Operational profiles are used for systems that can be described as state machines, or systems that have state-based behavior. An operational profile describes the probabilities of input in relation to the state of the system. The preparation of test cases is based on the distribution of these probabilities. [BN02]

In model-based testing[UL06], statistical test generation is often used to generate test sequences from environment models because it is the environment that determines the usage patterns of the SUT. A typical approach is to use a Markov chain to specify the expected usage profile of the SUT. A Markov chain is essentially an FSM with probabilities attached to the transitions. Test cases can be generated via a random walkthrough of the Markov chain, where the random choice of the next transition is made using the probability distribution of the outgoing transitions. This means that the test cases with greatest probability are likely to be generated first. In this approach, the usage model is a representation of the system use not its behavior. The usage model does not provide the expected response of the system; that is, no oracles are generated. With just a usage model, the oracle information has to be provided independently, either manually for each test case or by giving some general oracle criterion such as "no exceptions allowed," or "all output values must be in the range 10 .. 100." Another approach is to use this kind of statistical usage model (e.g., Markov chains) in addition to a behavioral model of the SUT. The statistical model acts as the test selection criterion and chooses the paths through the behavioral model while the behavioral model is used to generate the oracle information for those paths. This generates a test suite that can not only perform accurate oracle checking but also follow the expected usage profile of the SUT.

6.4.1 Statistical Usage Testing

Statistical usage testing is a way to derive test cases for system level black-box testing from the specification models. [HPR03] states that "taking the specification models as the basis for tests has the positive side effect that more attention is paid to keep the models complete and up-to-date. Another advantage is that testing can start in very early phases of the development process which is important for incremental development and allows to shorten the time to delivery. Furthermore the software quality is raised because the system is tested with respect to the explicitly stated user requirements."

State machines and usage graphs are very similar. Hence most model elements of a state machine can be transformed straight forward into corresponding elements in the usage graph. The basis for creating test cases in statistical usage testing is a usage model.

A usage model is a directed usage graph consisting of states and transitions, with the extension that every state transition is attributed to the probability that this transition will be traversed when the system is in the state from which the transition arc starts. Hence for every state the probabilities of outgoing transitions sum up to one. Every transition can be related to an event (possibly with parameters) which triggers that transition. A transition with an associated event may also be related to a guard condition. This means that the transition is only performed if the condition is fulfilled by the event parameter value(s).

There are three approaches [HPR03] to assign transition probabilities.

1. In the **uninformed approach** all exit arcs of a state have the same probability.

2. The **informed approach** uses sample user event sequences captured from a prototype or a prior version of the system to calculate suitable probabilities.

3. The **intended approach** allows to model hypothetic users or to shift the test focus to certain states or transitions.

The Marcov property states that all transition probabilities depend only on the actual state and are independent of the history, which means that they must be fixed numbers. A system with this property is called a Marcov chain, for which some valuable analytical descriptions can be concluded. One such description is the usage distribution stating the steady-state probability for every state, i.e. the expected appearance rate of that state. Since each state is associated with some part of the actual software, the usage distribution shows which parts of the software get most attention from the test cases. Other important descriptions are the expected test case length and the number of test cases that are necessary to verify the required reliability of the system. [HPR03]

6.4.2 Phases of Statistical Testing

The process of statistical testing based on a usage model can be divided into five phases[Pro03]:

1. Usage Modeling, where one or more usage models are constructed to represent the population of uses.

2. Model Analysis and Validation, in which usage models are analyzed to determine their properties, which are then compared against known or assumed properties of field use and test constraints.

3. Test Planning, where test cases are generated and test automation is planned and designed.

4. Test Execution, where the generated tests are executed against the system under test and the results are recorded.

5. Product and Process Measurement, where the results of the test are analyzed to determine expected reliability.

Throughout this process, there are opportunities for automation. For this reason, the Java Usage Model Builder Library (JUMBL) has been developed by the Software Quality Research Laboratory of the University of Tennessee.

6.4.3 Statistical Testing using JUMBL

In order to apply statistical testing, a usage model is developed and analyzed to validate its fitness for use in testing. As mentioned earlier, a usage model is a specification of the system's use not its behavior. In other words, the model represents what the user is likely to do next, not the internal states of the system. The model may then be used to generate test cases representing expected usage and to reason about system reliability given the performance on the set of tests. The Java Usage Model Builder Library (JUMBL) is a Java class library and set of command-line tools for working with usage models. The JUMBL supports construction and analysis of models, generation of test cases, automated execution of tests, and analysis of testing results.[Pro03] The most common format for developing usage models is The Model Language (TML) (figure 6.3), which is a simple language developed specifically for Markov chain usage models. The TML language supports developing usage models as compositions of other models to simplify specifying the structure of large models. For example, one might create a model of each user dialog presented by a software system and then create a top-level model which links these together. TML allows specifying the probabilities as constraints along with simple objective functions to simplify specifying the probability distribution for a usage model. For example, one might specify that one arc is twice as likely as another, and then leave all other arcs unconstrained. The JUMBL then chooses probabilities which honor the given constraints. Additionally, multiple distributions (as constraints) can be stored in a single model, and automated testing information (called labels) can be attached to parts of the model as necessary.[Pro03] "In addition to TML standard formats supported by the JUMBL include comma-separated value (CSV), the DOT language used by the Graphviz tools, GML as used by Graphlet, and Model Markup Language (MML). MML is an XML extension language created specifically for representing Markov chain usage models."[Pro03]

The JUMBL creates a comprehensive analytical report of model and use statistics which can be used to validate model correctness, plan for testing, investigate expected use, and compare different modeling approaches.[Pro03]

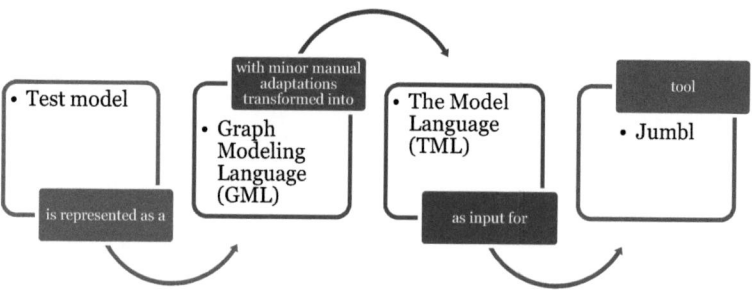

Figure 6.3: Steps before using the tool JUMBL

6.4.4 Test Generation using JUMBL

The JUMBL can generate test cases in five ways[Pro03]:

- A collection of test cases can be generated covering the model with minimum cost.
- Test cases can be generated by random sampling with replacement. Test cases can be generated in order of probability.
- There is an interactive test case editor for creating test cases by hand.
- Test cases can be created by interleaving the events of other test cases.

6.5 State Charts (SCs)

The Unified Modeling Language (UML) is now the standard used for modeling in software engineering. As mentioned earlier, UML 2.2 has 14 types of diagrams divided into two categories. Seven diagram types represent structural information, and the other seven represent general types of behavior, including four that represent different aspects of interactions. In this thesis, State Charts are chosen since they are the primary means within the UML for capturing complex dynamic behavior.

A State Chart shows the possible states and the transitions that cause a change in state. From each state comes a complete set of transitions that determine the subsequent state. States are rounded rectangles. Transitions are arrows from one state to another. Events or conditions that trigger transitions are written beside the arrows. The action that occurs as a result of an event or condition is expressed in the form event/action.

Figure 6.4 represents the main contents that will appear in the Colored State Chart.

In the latest version of UML, the UML state machines unfortunately do not offer operators,

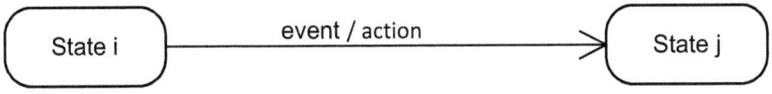

Figure 6.4: A State Chart

sub-languages and/or graphical notations for specifying product lines.[LG08] Therefore, in order to overcome this obstacle, it is targeted to extend the UML state diagrams to represent the product lines and the variability.

6.6 Why State Charts?

The intention of this section is to shed light on how much more concise and structured the State Chart version is in comparison to the natural language specifications.

6.6.1 Why not Natural Language Specifications?

Although the behavior of a URC may be intuitive to describe, the behavior of such an application in natural language can be surprisingly difficult. Most specifications written for real projects try to be detailed as much as possible, but they usually leave many aspects of a system unspecified and open to interpretations. Even if a serious attempt is made to specify a system in detail, it is almost impossible to write one without ambiguity, inconsistency, incompleteness and redundancy. Thus, one of the main problems with using natural languages for specifications is their inherent ambiguity. The semantics of each word is not well defined and when words are combined into sentences and paragraphs, the ambiguity can be magnified further. Even when precise and accurate descriptions are used, they are often very long and difficult to understand. The best way to capture the precise behavior is to produce a model of the targeted behavior in a graphical language that has well-defined semantics. The advantage of this approach is that many of the problems with natural language specifications are avoided. [Hor99]

6.6.2 Advantages of State Charts

The use of state machines is widespread in the electronics industry.[Hor99] More specifically, State Charts are a well known design method to develop embedded systems. They have been chosen for modeling the product line test model for the following reasons and advantages[Mue09][Gom10]:

- Many embedded systems consist of multiple threads, each running an FSM. State charts allow the modeling of these parallel threads

- State Charts allow designing the dynamic behavior of a device. Parts of an embedded device can be often modeled as state machine due to the reactive nature of embedded devices. Devices react to some kind of external or internal stimuli which lead to an action and, eventually, to a change of state.

- A state machine forces the programmer to think of all the cases and, therefore, to extract all the required information from the user. One can quickly draw a state transition diagram on a whiteboard, in front of the user, and walk him through it. The first and hardest step is to figure out what the user really wants the software to do.

- State Charts provide a good level of abstraction: Many people with different technical background understand State Chart diagrams. This is important because for the development of an embedded system often different engineering disciplines come together. Therefore, State Charts are a very good basis to discuss the modeled behavior or requirements in design reviews with colleagues or customers.

- State Charts allow finding defects already in the design phase. To decrease cost of poor quality, it is important to find defects as early as possible in the development process. During the design, usually defects related to unclear, incomplete or missing requirements are found. Such defects can lead to very costly redesigns or even to the reconstruction of the system if they are found not before the system test. State Charts open a number of possibilities to find defects early in the process.

- State Charts allow simulation of the modelled behaviour: It is easily possible to execute a State Chart in a simulator and allow the user to send events to the machine and observe how the State Chart reacts to the sent stimuli. This way the user can interactively test the model and improve it where necessary.

- Robustness of state charts can be automatically checked on model level: In the hardware design automatic design rule checks are very common. For software designs, this is not yet common. Software design rules need to be defined; handmade checks are time-consuming and the result is very dependent on the reviewer. In practice, a tool is needed to ensure that checks are really performed.

- Automatic code-generation reduces coding errors: Once the state chart was checked the implementation can start. It is highly recommended not to code the state machine by hand but let a tool generate the code for you. Automatic code generation has many benefits especially if a model checker is integrated in the generator and can perform a large number of checks automatically. Especially composite state charts can be tricky to code by hand. When transitions or states have to be added because of an additional requirement one wishes to have a generator at hand taking over all the error-prone placement of entry, exit and action code associated with states or transitions.

- Automatically deriving test-cases from the model: There are several articles about testing state machines, but the one written by Martin Gomez [Gom10] summarizes the usually used approach:

"The beauty of coding even simple algorithms as state machines is that the test plan almost writes itself. All you have to do is to go through every state transition. I usually do it with a highlighter in hand, crossing off the arrows on the state transition diagram as they successfully pass their tests ... This requires a fair amount of patience and coffee, because even a mid-size state machine can have 100 different transitions. However, the number of transitions is an excellent measure of the system's complexity."

Based on a state chart model the tool JUMBL, introduced later can take over this time consuming manual task of defining routes through the state chart ensuring 100% transition coverage. Implementing the test cases is a task that one still has to do. But a good code generator can also support by automatically generating trace code if needed for test purposes.

In the next chapter the CMBT-SWPL using the CSC is represented, where only one State Chart is depicted that captures all product line variants.

Chapter 7

Colored Model Based Testing for Software Product Lines (CMBT-SWPL)

> "Success is not the key to happiness. Happiness is the key to success. If you love what you are doing, you will be successful." Albert Schweitzer

7.1 Introduction

This chapter introduces the concept of the Colored State Chart(CSC), followed by in-depth details on how testing for embedded product lines is conducted using the CMBT-SWPL method. The transformation from CSC to CPN for verification and simulation purposes is then presented. Next, the tool PENECA Chromos is introduced followed by an explanation of simulation in terms of concept and function.

7.2 Colored State Charts (CSCs)

State Charts (SCs) used here are based on David Harel´s State Charts introduced in 1987[Har87]. They were later incorporated into the UML [OMG09], followed by some modifications and an object-oriented interpretation. The basics of the State Charts are covered in [Fow03], [OMG09] as "UML state machine diagrams".

UML State Charts cannot address product lines. Thus, the extended State Chart version as introduced in [FFD02], [FFDD02] and [Fen04], will be used in the present work to address product lines. Such State Charts are called "Colored State Charts" (referred to as CSC) and are based on the basic idea of Colored Petri Nets (CPNs), as described in [Jen80] or [Fen93].

The basic principle is based on the folding of similar state diagrams, which represent, for example, a class and its subclasses, or more object instances of a class. In figure 7.1 an example is depicted to explain the idea.

7.2.1 Example: Folding of States and Transitions

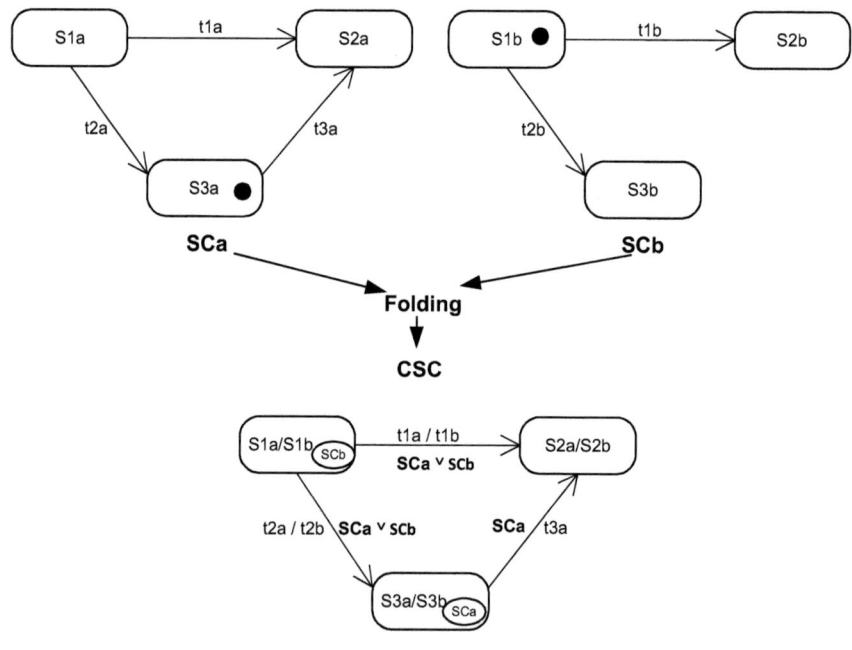

Figure 7.1: Folding of States and Transitions (from [FFDD02])

In this example, State Charts SCa and SCb have the same states, but differ only in the transitions. SCa and SCb have the transitions t1a and t1b respectively as well as t2a and t2b. However, t3a exists only in SCa. The included tokens (black dots) in S3a and S1b show the currently active states in the state diagrams SCa and SCb. Tokens move when transitions fire into the next active state. In the resulting CSC, the common states and transitions are superimposed. This superimposition is labeled as shown in figure 7.1. For example, the two states S1a and S1b will be superimposed in the CSC to S1a/S1b and correspondingly the two transitions t1a and t1b are superimposed in the CSC to t1a/t1b. The states or transitions (e.g. t3a) that are only present in one state diagram are transferred to the CSC. In the CSC, the tokens SCa and SCb appear in the states (S1a/S1b and S3a/S3b), as a result of the superimposition of the corresponding marked states in SCa or SCb. The transitions of the CSC will be further labeled with the disjunction of the SC names, which are involved in the superimposition of the transitions. For example, the transition arising from t1a and t1b will be labeled $SCa \lor SCb$ and the transition arising from only t3a will be labeled SCa. The SCi names used in the tokens and on the transitions are described in the following sections as colors. Transitions can fire, if the originating state contains a token of color SCi (e.g. S1a/S1b contains the token SCb) and the disjunction of the transition contains SCi (e.g. the disjunction of t2a/t2b contains SCb).

7.2.2 Formal Definitions

The CSC in figure 7.1 will be depicted in the overall following figure 7.2. The following CSC used does not use all the options mentioned in [FFDD02],[FFD02] and [Fen04]. In order to extend the State Chart (SC) to a Colored State Chart (CSC) based on the general State Chart definition, the present work will focus only on the following:

- S: a finite set of complex states.
- The elements of S are called s.
- T: a finite number of complex transitions with $T \subseteq S \times S$.
- The elements of T are resulting as (si, sj).

In addition, the following is introduced:

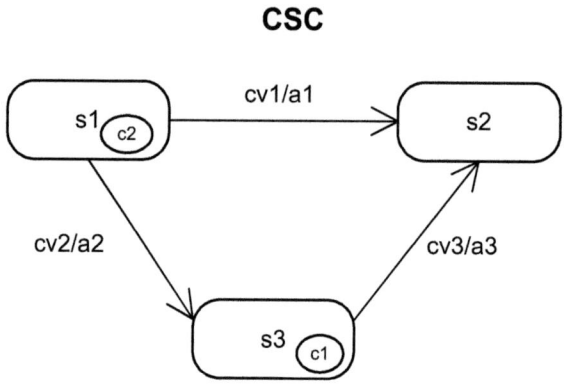

```
cvd(cv1) = (c1 , c2)      s1 : S1a / S1b        c1 : SCa
cvd(cv2) = (c1 , c2)      s2 : S2a / S2b        c2 : SCb
cvd(cv3) = (c1)           s3 : S3a / S3b
ai represents actions
```

Figure 7.2: Example of a Colored State Chart(CSC)

- C: a finite set of colors.
- The elements of C are called c.
- CV: a finite set of color variables.
- The elements of CV are called cv.
- m: a marking with m: $S \to P(C)$, were P(C) is the power set of C.
- ctf: a color transition function with $T \to CV$.
- For each $cv \in CV$ belongs a definition set cvd with $cvd \subseteq C \land cvd \neq \emptyset$.

For the state transitions in the CSC, there is a transition firing rule:

- A transition (si, sj) can fire for $c \in C$ if $c \in m(si)$.

- A transition fires for $c \in C$ if and only if it can fire for c (and additionally the events and the guards of the transition are fulfilled).

The result of firing of (si,sj) for $c \in C$ is:

- $m^{k+1}(si) = m^k(si)\setminus\{c\}$ and $m^{k+1}(sj) = m^k(sj) \cup \{c\}$

- k is before firing (si, sj); k +1 is after firing (si, sj).

- A transition fires in parallel for different colors, if it can fire for these colors.

Colored State Charts can be transformed to Colored Petri Nets [FFDD02]. This makes verification of the transformed model possible using widespread methods and tools developed for CPN.

7.3 Testing Product Lines with CMBT-SWPL Method

7.3.1 CMBT-SWPL : Domain Engineering.

Within the domain engineering (the left part of figure 7.3) of the product line a feature model was developed in [Die03] to model the variable and common features of the product line. For further elaboration of the example the present work will mainly concentrate on the features shown in figure 7.4, referenced as "Reduced Feature Model". The selection of features in the reduced feature model for a certain product line variant is called feature configuration. In parallel to the feature model, a usage model is developed, represented as State Chart with usage probabilities. It models the black box usage of the system and is extended towards a Colored State Chart. From (figure 7.4), several product line variants could be extracted. For simplification purposes the focus will be in the following definitions on only three product line variants (see figure 7.7), (figure 7.8) and (figure 7.9).

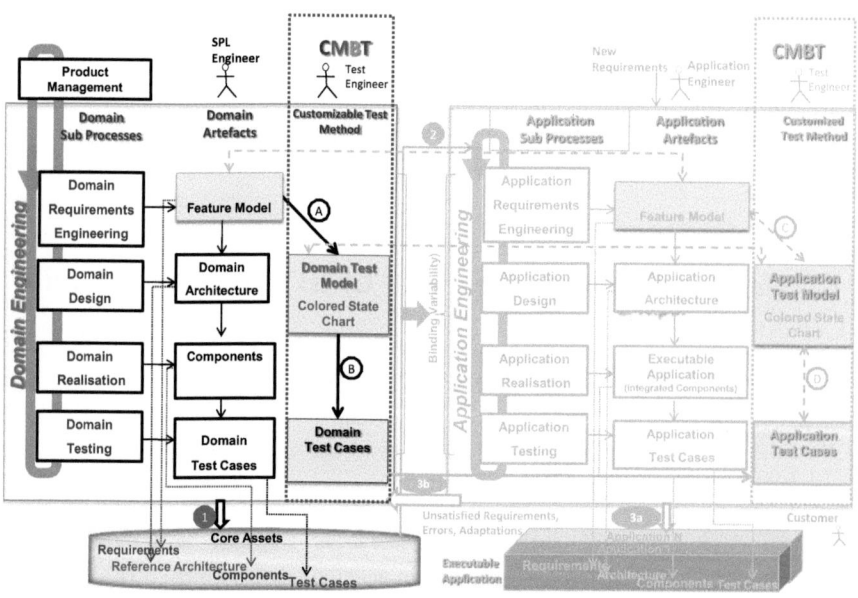

Figure 7.3: Colored Model-Based Testing for Software Product Lines(CMBT-SWPL) - Domain Engineering

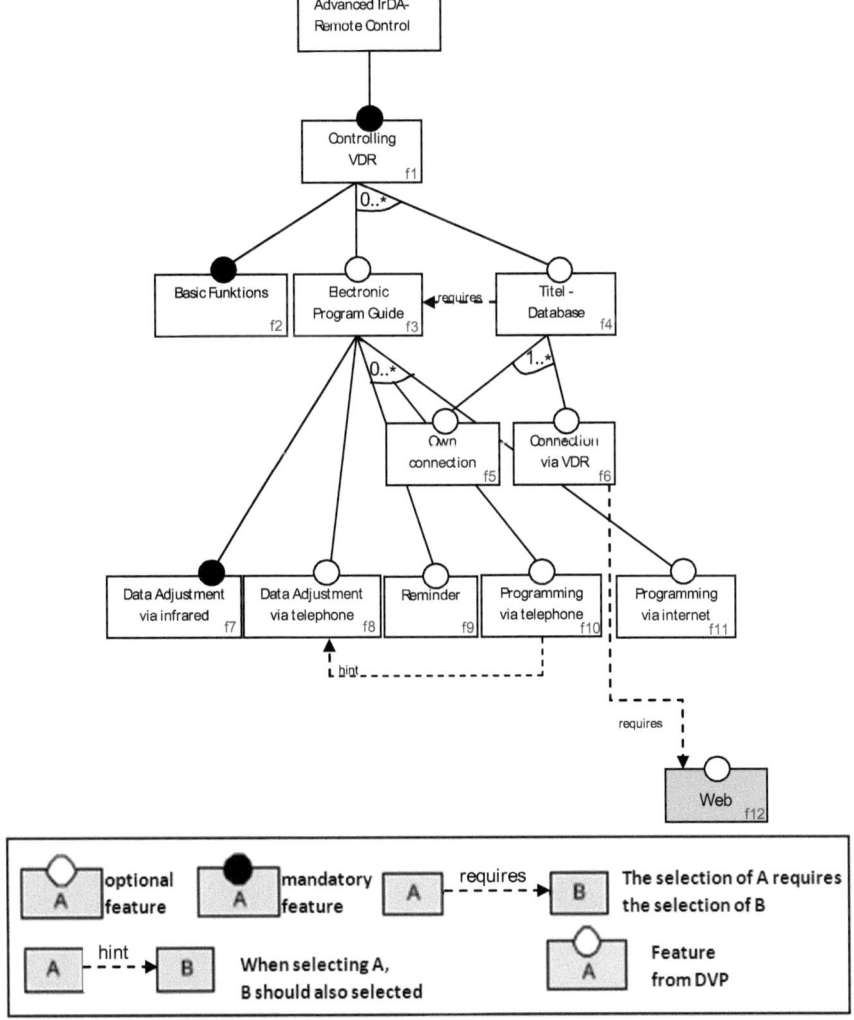

Figure 7.4: Reduced Feature Model

Those three product line variants are defined in figure 7.5:

$VD(v1) = \{f1, f2\}$

(f1 = Basic Functions)

$VD(v2) = \{f1, f2, f3\}$

(f1 = Basic Functions, f2 = Electronic Program Guide(EPG))

$VD(v3) = \{f1, f2, f3, f9\}$

(f1 = Controlling VDR, f2 = Basic Functions, f3 = Electronic Program Guide(EPG), f9 = Reminder)

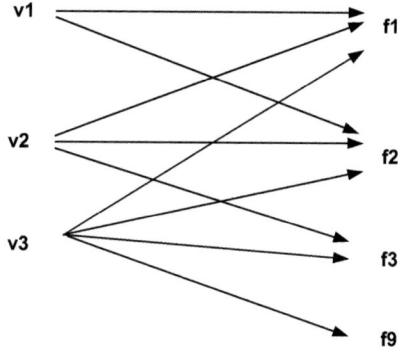

Figure 7.5: Product Line Variants to Features Assignments

- F represents the set of all features and corresponds to CV from section 7.2.2

  The elements of F are called f and build the color variables in CSC of figure 7.6

- V represents the set of all defined product line variants and is equivalent to C from section 7.2.2

  The elements of V are called v and build the colors in CSC in figure 7.6.

- VD is the variant definition set. VD contains the allocation of all defined product line variants to the features and is produced from the specification of the product line variants and the restrictions of the feature model.

- $(VD : V \rightarrow F)$

- $(VD(v) = \{fi, fj, fk, \ldots\}$

The reduced feature model results in three product line variants (V1, V2 and V3). V1 includes features f1 and f2. V2 includes features f1, f2 and f3. V3 includes features f1, f2, f3 and f9. The set of all features corresponds to the finite set of color variables of the colored State Chart. The features correspond to the color variables, presented in the test model in figure 7.6.

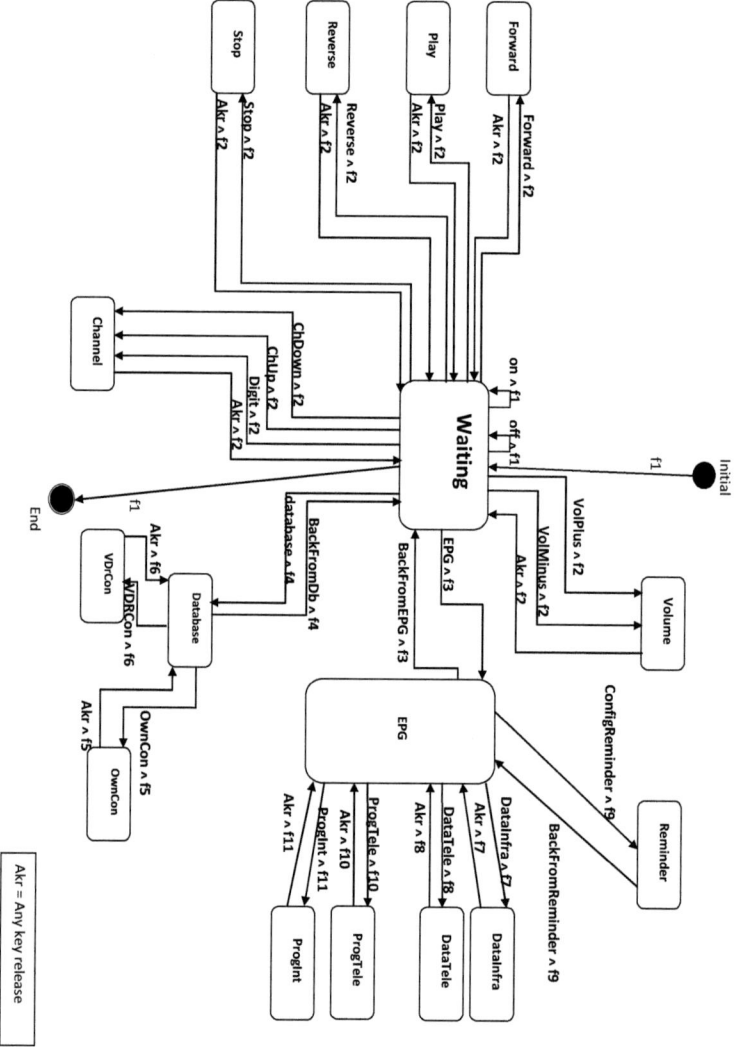

Figure 7.6: CSC-Test Model

CHAPTER 7

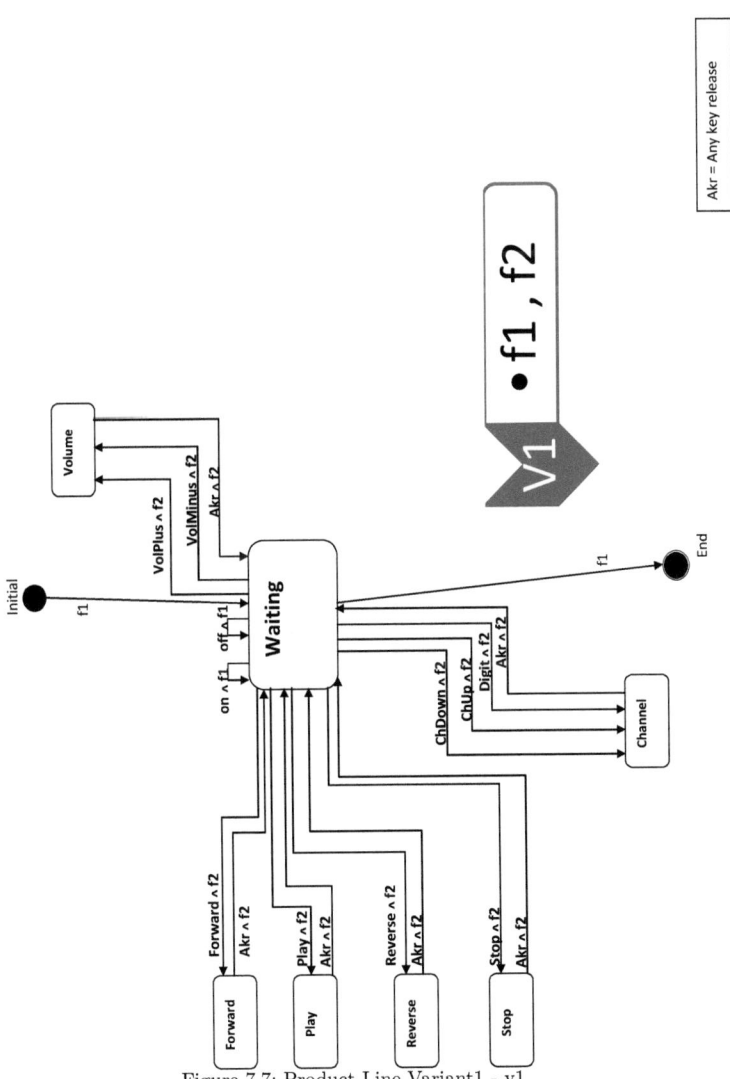

Figure 7.7: Product Line Variant1 - v1

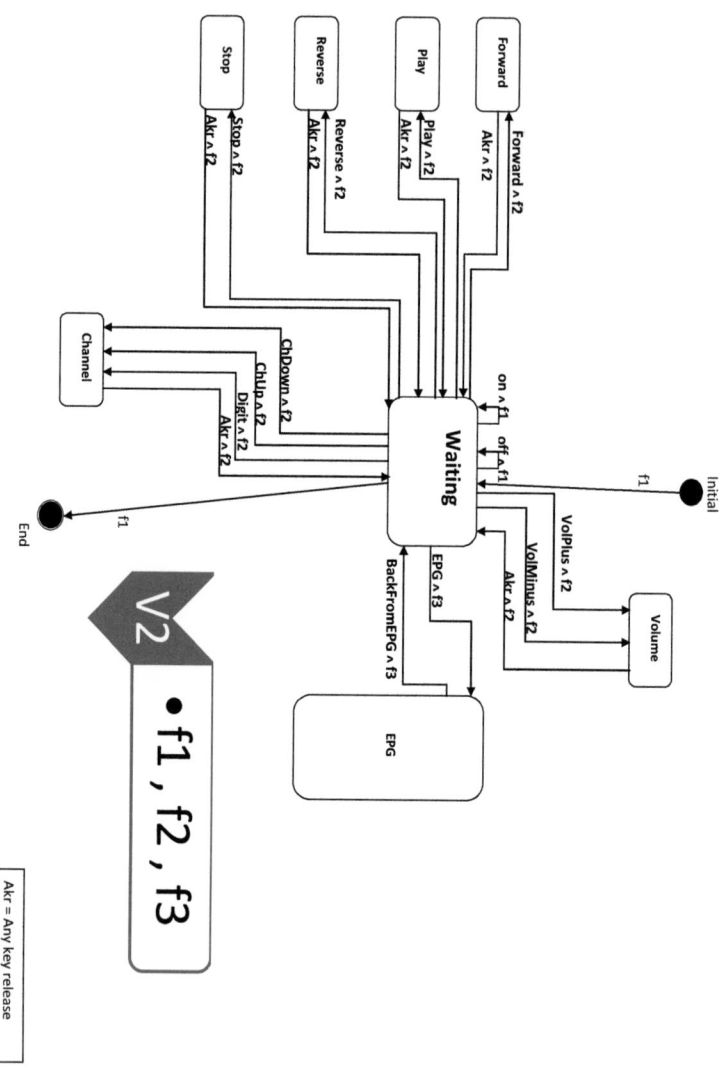

Figure 7.8: Product Line Variant2 - v2

CHAPTER 7

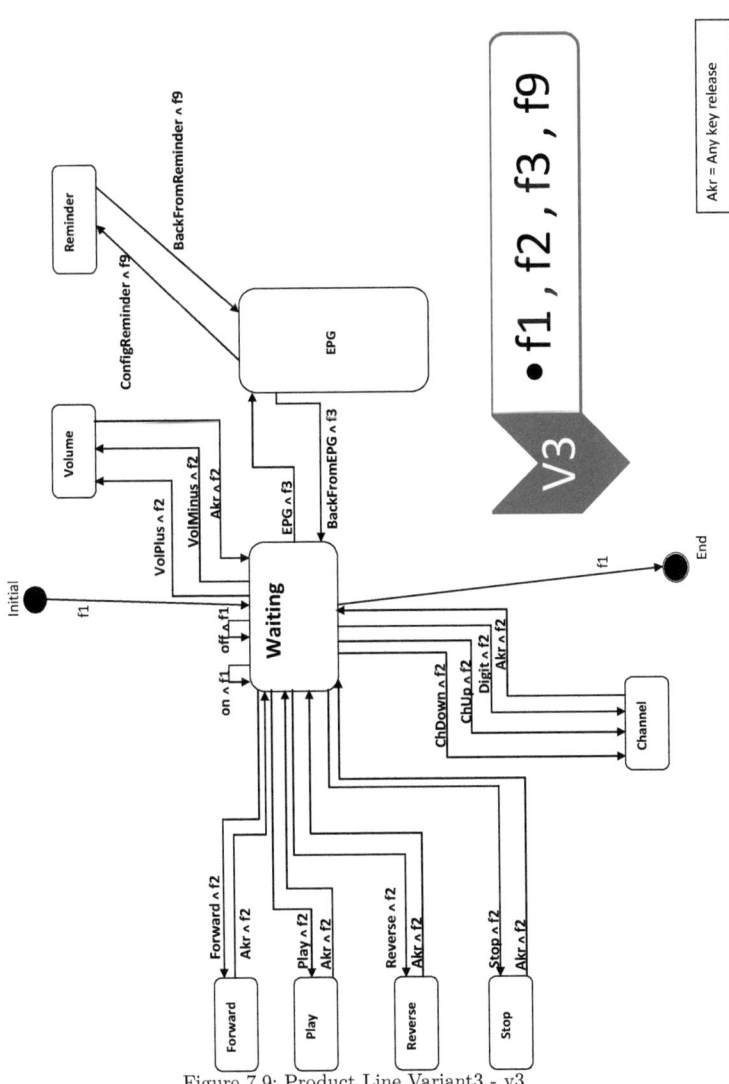

Figure 7.9: Product Line Variant3 - v3

This test model can be elaborated formally as explained in the following lines and based on Section 7.2.2:

- S represents the set of all states.
- Symbolic identifiers are used for the elements of S.
- $S = \{Waiting, Volume, \ldots\}$
- T represents the set of all transitions.
- The elements of T are resulting from $S \times S$ as (symbolic identifier i, symbolic identifier j)
- $T = \{(Waiting, Volume), (Waiting, Waiting), \ldots\}$

   An example for a condition is:

- $condition(Waiting, Volume) = VolPlus$

   An example for cft is:

- cft(Waiting, Volume) = f2

   The set of features is:

- $F = CV = \{f1, f2, f3, f4, f5, f6, f7, f8, f9, f10, f11, f12\}$

   The set of the defined product line variant is:

- $V = C = \{v1, v2, v3\}$ From the VD(v), the assignment of the product line variant vi to the feature fj can be directly derived as following:

- $cvd(f1) = \{v1, v2, v3\}$
- $cvd(f2) = \{v1, v2, v3\}$
- $cvd(f3) = \{v2, v3\}$
- $cvd(f9) = \{v3\}$

Based on the knowledge captured in the feature model and the previously developed usage model a CSC is developed (see (A) in figure 7.3). The CSC includes the behavior of the system family and its variability as well, represented by the colors. At any given moment, the CSC refers to one active product line variant while the remaining variants are passive. This is similar to the concept of instantiation in the object oriented paradigm. One active product variant is equivalent to a certain feature configuration extracted from the feature diagram or from the CSC.

One color, i.e. one product line variant may consist of one or more features, in this case color variables (figure 7.10). Within the domain test model in (figure 7.6), variability is realized by mapping the features to one or more transitions (figure 7.11). The events are combined with features present in a given application of the product line. A transition will only be able to fire if all features which are bound to it are present in the derived application.

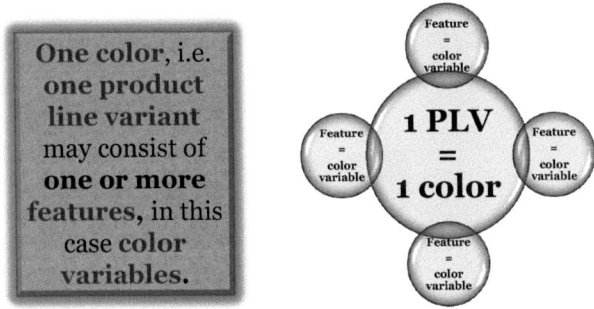

Figure 7.10: One product line variant constitute of one or more features

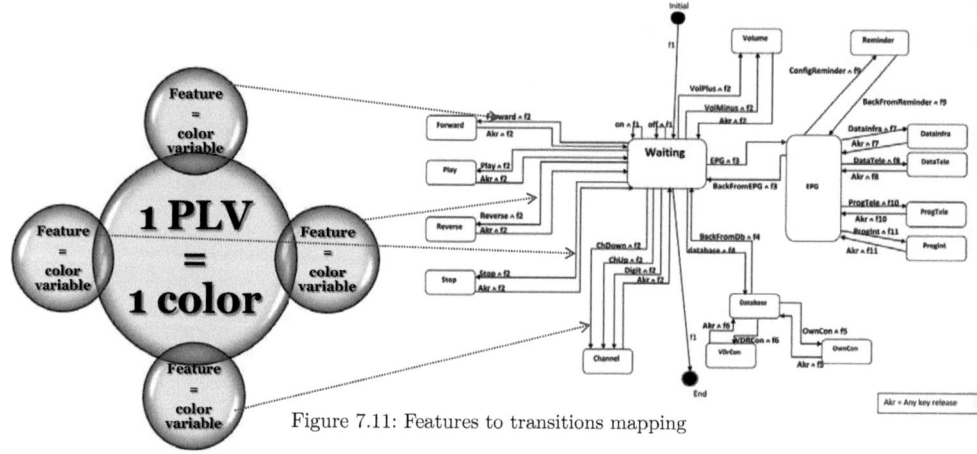

Figure 7.11: Features to transitions mapping

The domain test model includes all features of the product line. Out of the domain test model, domain test cases (see (B) in figure 7.3) are derived (see figure 7.13) by reducing the feature set to the common features, which is the core of the product line. Based on this reduction, a State Chart is derived and enhanced with usage probabilities to be used as input for the generation of test cases, described in section 7.3.3. The test artifacts (see figure 7.12) gained until this step such as test models and test cases are stored in the repository to be reused for the derivation of applications of the product line.

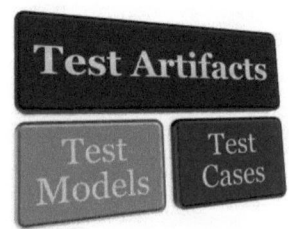

Figure 7.12: Test Artifacts

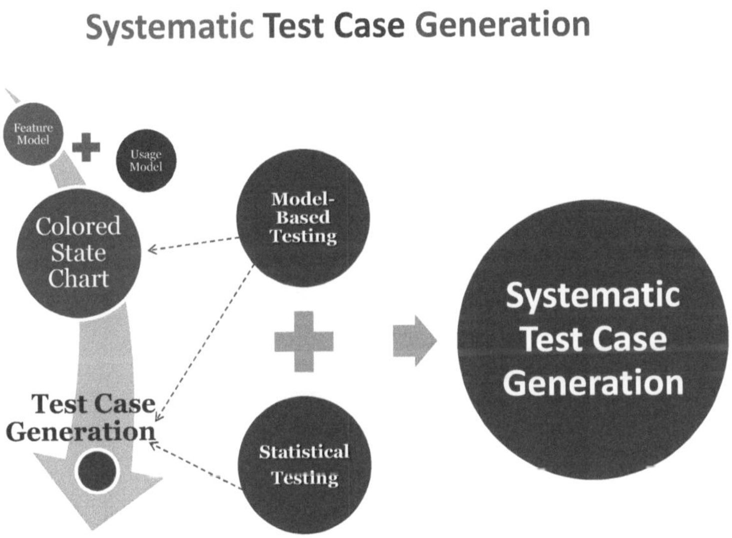

Figure 7.13: Systematic Test Case Generation

7.3.2 CMBT-SWPL : Application Engineering

Within the application engineering (the right part of figure 7.14) of the product line, the feature model is reused. Based on the Application Requirements Engineering phase, possible required changes to the feature model are thoroughly assessed. In case such new requirements make changing the feature model worthwhile, these changes are fed back to the Domain Engineering phase. The next step is to customise the colored domain test model (i.e. one color is chosen) to produce the colored application test model for a specific application (see (C) in figure 7.14). The CSC is transformed into a State Chart modeling the behavior of a single application and enhanced with usage probabilities to generate test cases (see (D) in figure 7.14) for this application using the statistical testing approach described in section 7.3.3. Traceability information (depicted by the dotted arrows) created during the first activities are required to perform activity D.

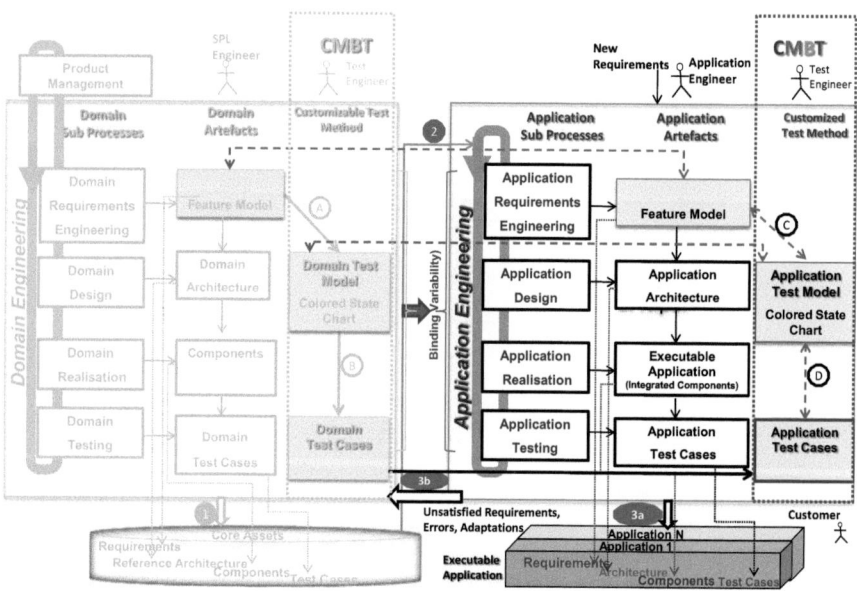

Figure 7.14: Colored Model-Based Testing for Software Product Lines(CMBT-SWPL) - Application Engineering

Statistical testing as one of the technologies to reduce the huge test space, was chosen based on own experiences in the embedded software development domain, expert knowledge of embedded software developers in the automation domain and the results of the D-MINT project. Other approaches towards test case reduction and generation are subject of further research.

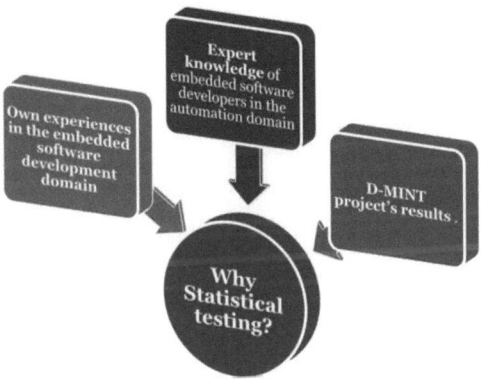

Figure 7.15: Why Statistical Testing?

7.3.3 Statistical Testing

Statistical testing [Poo00], [WT94] is based on usage models. Such models represent the typical (based on statistics) usage of a system, in our case by an end user. The usage model may be expressed by a State Chart with annotated transition probabilities. All possible paths from the start to the final state form the test cases of the system.

As depicted in figure 7.16 (a), each test case is composed of the transitions and states along a path from the start to the final state. Part (a) of the figure results in a test case along the transitions goto_A, goto_AC, goto_CF and goto_X in exactly this order. For each transition, test steps according to a test interface are defined, e.g. push buttons on the system under test (SUT) or the measurement of the reference values parallel to the test case execution. As shown in (b) of figure 7.16, circular paths of transitions are possible, e.g. increase in volume by one step, which results in different volume levels according to the number of circulations per test case. Clearly, an abort criterion is needed to exit such circular paths to generate test cases for such a State Chart (note: the volume example needs to have an upper bound which is left out of the discussion). In statistical testing, this abort criterion is addressed by probabilities attached to the transitions of the State Chart.

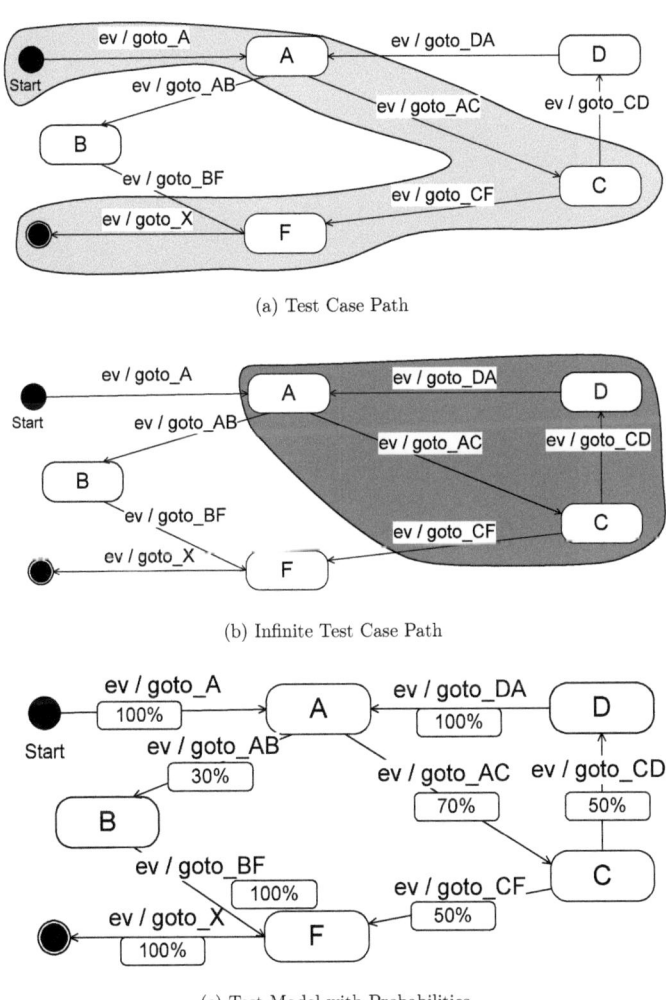

Figure 7.16: Statistical Testing based on Usage Models

Finally, in part (c) of figure 7.16 the probabilities conform to (figure 7.17) the usage of the system, which can be obtained by observing the user using the system, using similar project´s statistics or by expert estimations which can be further refined if necessary through usage.

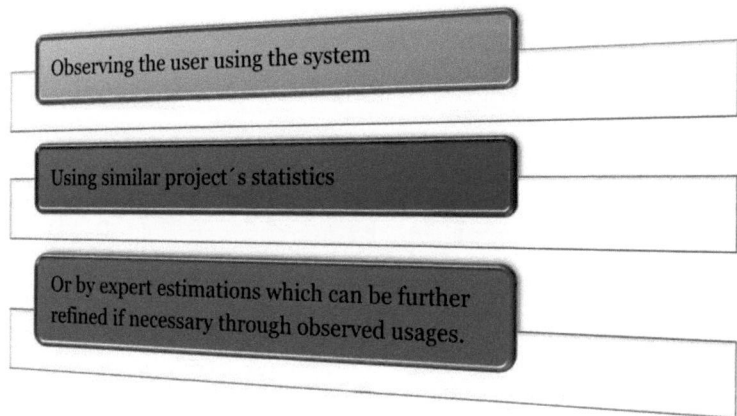

Figure 7.17: How is the typical usage obtained?

In part (c) of figure 7.16, 70% of the cases users of the system would change from state A to state C, in 30% from A to B, according to the annotated probabilities. Based on the State Chart with probabilities, test cases are generated, e.g. with full state and/or transition coverage with the least possible paths. Alternatively, a given number of test cases may be generated according to the probabilities.

The tool JUMBL [Pro03] is used to generate test cases according to the above mentioned criteria. The test model in 7.16 is presented as Graph Modeling Language (GML) with minor manual adaptations transformed into The Model Language (TML) used as input for JUMBL (figure 6.3).

7.4 Colored Petri Nets (CPN)

This section shows the result of transforming the CSC (figure 7.6 on page 108) of the universal remote control example to a CPN (see figure 7.18, 7.19, 7.20) for verification and simulation purposes. It is worth of note that the label edges of the CPN arise from color variables of the CSC.

7.5 PENECA Chromos

In the next section PENECA Chromos[Wik96]is used as a tool (figure 7.21) for design and simulation of Petri Nets. It has been developed at the Technical University of Ilmenau in corporation with OWIS Software GmbH, Martinroda. This tool includes an interface to the analysing tool INA and a component for statistical evaluation. This statistical component allows observation and recording of the net's firing behaviour.[DMMF97]

7.6 Simulation

By using the animated Petri Net simulation tool "PENECA Chromos", the designer can observe the effects of changes by simple manipulations in the model. The developer is enabled to experiment with variations in order to see the effects of particular changes. The simulation tool immediately interprets the net in it's actual state and changes can be performed rapidly without the need to write any line of code. If one is given an animation component, the results can be visualized in a clear and easy to understand way. Decisions show their consequences in an immediate manner. This intuitive approach leads to faster development, makes it easier to find solutions for a problem and avoid disadvantageous decisions. In this study's example, simulation was helpful and without it, errors would not have been traced immediately. The clearly visible differences during simulation lead to rapid error correction. Simulation can be used to predict quantitative properties of the process, especially statistical ones. Such measurements are valid with respect to the chosen stimulus parameters, which may be varied to get additional information.[DMMF97]

CHAPTER 7

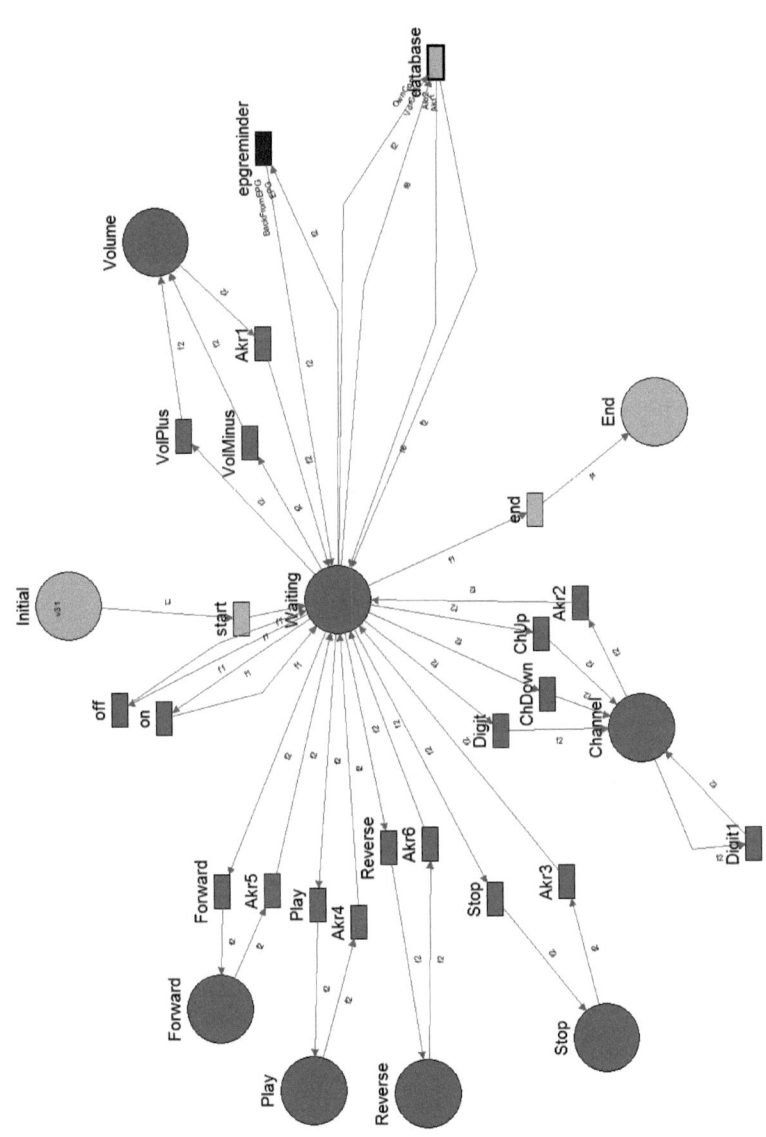

Figure 7.18: Petri Net 1

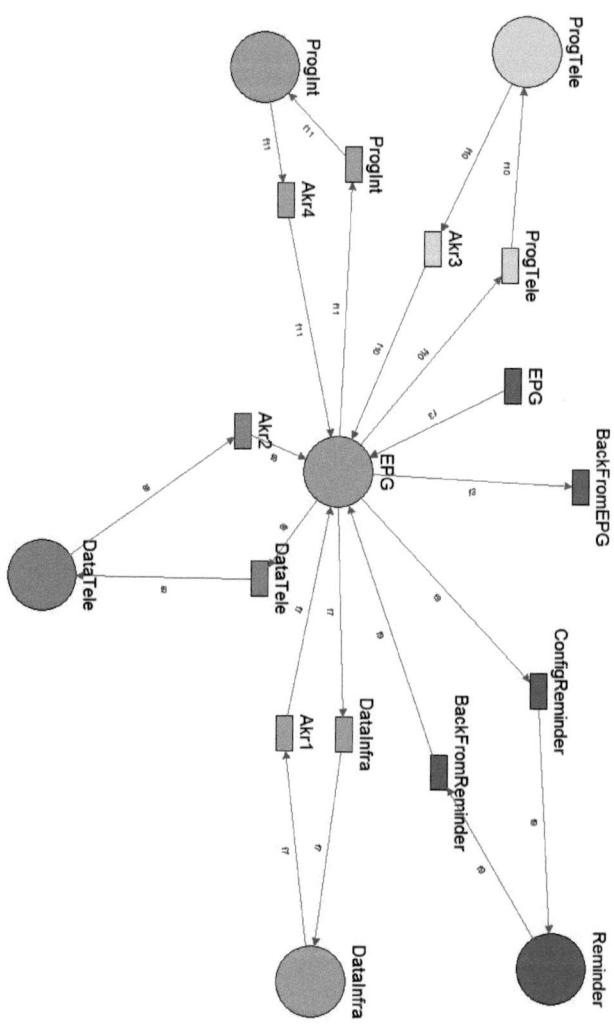

Figure 7.19: Petri Net 2

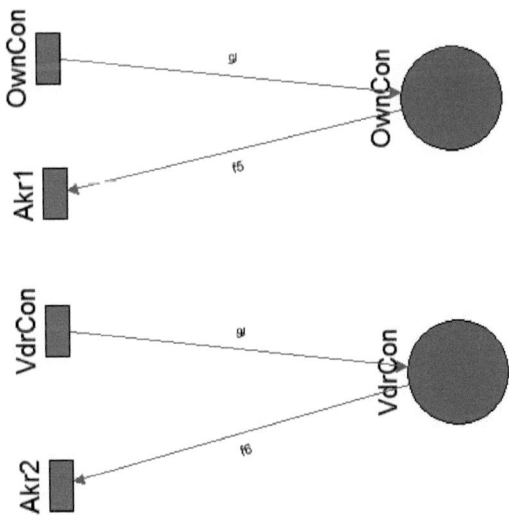

Figure 7.20: Petri Net 3

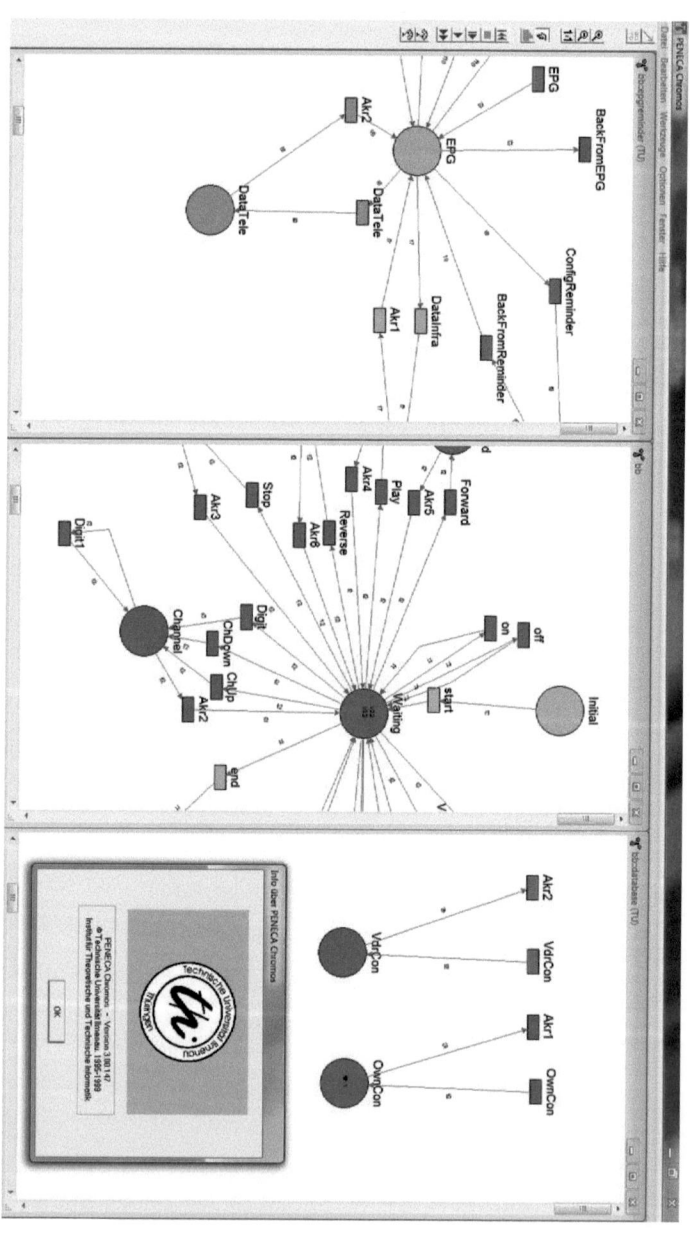

Figure 7.21: PENECA Chromos

Chapter 8

Evaluation

"The only way of finding the limits of the possible is by going beyond them into the impossible." Arthur C. Clarke

8.1 Introduction

Software product line engineering needs an appropriate test model to complete the whole product engineering. The presented approach supports the reuse of Colored State Charts, i.e. the test models. This reuse of the test models and the automatic test generation indicate that the test effort can be saved by using the "Colored Model Based Testing for Software Product Lines lines" (CMBT-SWPL) method.

This reusable feature-oriented model-based testing method, namely CMBT-SWPL is used to create test assets from feature models, which can then be configured to test individual applications that are members of the software product line.

This method can be used to reduce the number of reusable test assets created to cover all features, and select feature combinations of a software product line. These test assets can be automatically selected and configured during application engineering to test a given application derived from the software product line.

8.2 Results

As mentioned before UML state machines do not consider product line variability. With the approach described in this thesis, variability will be considered early by introducing it directly in the main product line components of the CSC. Thus, by using the CSC, the product line variability can be extended to the UML state machines. Accordingly, variability is preserved in test cases as they are generated from colored test models automatically.

To sum up, one of the main benefits of the CMBT-SWPL method is its formal syntax as well as a formal semantic for the CSC and the consideration of variability.

As a result of the D-MINT project [DM10], an overall improvement of 35% (compared to a non-model based testing approach) for the testing development activities was achieved using model-based testing of single applications (statistical testing was a central part of this project) within the automation domain. Combining the CMBT-SWPL method to the statistical testing within the embedded product line domain is expected to lead to a reduction of test case development time, cost and effort by $\overline{4}5\%$ (based on interviews with domain experts).Future research will result in metrics on the improvement due to the CMBT-SWPL product line testing.

8.3 Colored Model Based Testing for Software Product Lines - Strong Points

The main two approaches that also address reuse and model based testing are ScenTED[RKPR05] and CADeT[Oli08] (figure 8.1). In this section, focus will be made on the main points that make CMBT-SWPL approach more advantageous as follows:

1. Compact presentation (CSC).

    - If they were not compact, then we would have to model several separate State Charts, then errors are more likely to occur in each individual model. The modelling effort for the CSC describing all product line features admittedly exceeds the effort needed for a state machine describing just one product variant. However, it requires a less considerable effort than modelling and maintaining an individual State Chart for each product variant of a product line, in particular, for large product lines with dozens of features.

CHAPTER 8

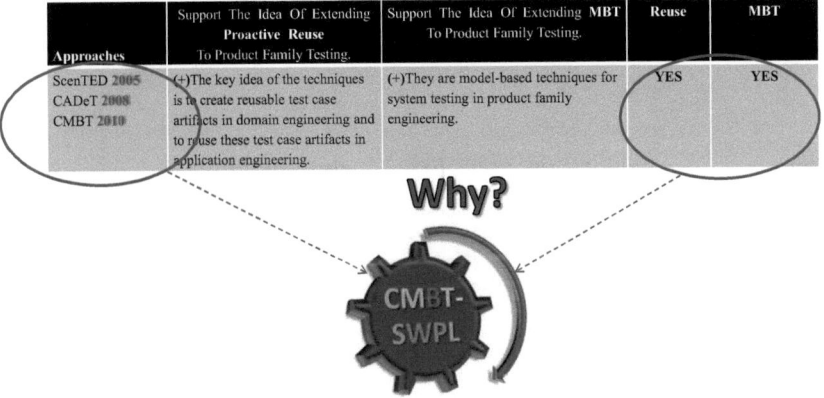

Figure 8.1: What makes CMBT-SWPL so special?

- On the other hand, when the developer will try to realize this compact presentation, he will try to avoid redundancies, ambiguities and incompleteness.

- The method provided compact presentation by representing all product line variants in one model, namely CSC. The developed test model is able to manage large numbers of feature combinations. Colors and tokens are used to distinguish between active and passive product line variants.

- Transformation from CSC to CPN is easily performed and accordingly achieve the benefits from CPN's Verification and Analysis Methods.
  Thus, product line's test artifacts are less complex, compact, expressive and helpful in modeling both simple and complex embedded reactive product lines.

2. Early Verification not only Validation of product lines.

    Product line verification is accomplished by transforming the CSC into a CPN utilizing the powerful analysis methods of PNs regarding for example how to deal with conflicts, deadlocks, and unwanted states. This helped in diagnosing and tracing the errors as it is performed in the Petri Nets approach.

3. More complex systems can be addressed by using State Charts, which are the most widespread suitable UML models used for modeling complex embedded product lines.

According to the above mentioned advantages, CMBT-SWPL is recommended to be the choice when testing a software product line.

8.4 Discussion

Using the CMBT-SWPL introduced in this thesis showed that the targeted goals have been achieved as follows:

- After comparing the new CMBT-SWPL method with the other testing product line methods, the CMBT-SWPL method is considerably simpler than the existing variants because:

    - The new method introduced the concept of colors.
    - It enables to manage complexity by a test model instead of many hundreds of manually defined test cases.
    - It automates test case generation and test result analysis.
    - It enables one-click verification of the test model (by Petri Net technologies)

- The CSC model is an economical way of dealing with the increasing complexity in the embedded product line domain. CMBT-SWPL seems to be powerful and expressive enough for modeling typical behavior and interaction requirements of systems in the embedded domain in an efficient way, reducing the development effort by 30%.

CHAPTER 8

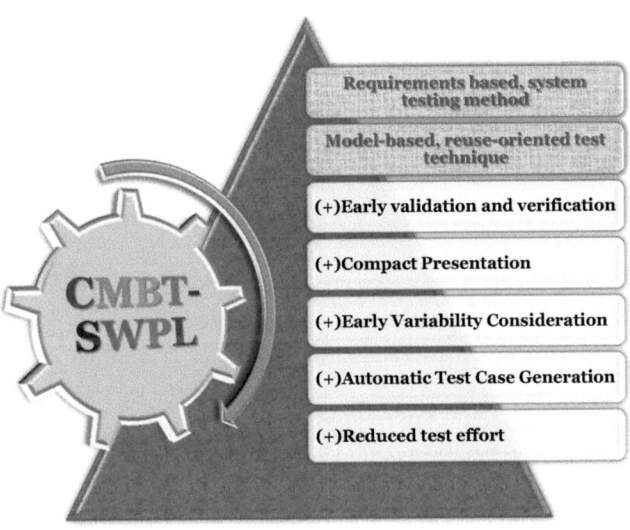

Figure 8.2: CMBT-SWPL Method

- Ambiguities, incompleteness, redundancies, etc. in requirements were addressed in an earlier stage when trying to achieve this compact presentation.

- By using the new principle of colors in State Chart, compact presentation through folding is possible, although this approach is fully maximized when used with the appropriate tool support.

- Variability, which is a basic concept in product lines, is introduced for the various test artifacts by using the principle of colors.

- The benefits of model based testing and statistical testing in the context of product lines are achieved because of the preserved variability in all test artifacts. More precisely, variability is introduced in the colored test model and accordingly in the test cases as they are generated using statistical testing form the reusable Colored

State Chart.

- The behavior captured in the CSC could be transformed to CPNs. The powerful verification and analysis methods of Petri Nets regarding for example how to deal with conflicts, deadlocks, and unwanted states, could be implemented.

- Furthermore, this transformation to CPNs facilitates the early validation of the method, which has been achieved by the simulation performed using PENECA Chromos.

- The product line infrastructure contains better tested reusable components, which result in a higher quality of the components.

Thus, the CMBT method provides an important step toward the goal of modeling increasingly complex semantics of UML State Charts in the context of embedded product lines.

Chapter 9

Conclusion

"Arriving at one goal is the starting point to another." John Dewey

In this chapter, a conclusion of the thesis is presented.

- Section 9.1: Provides a summary for the overall thesis layout, which discusses the main issues that motivated the thesis.
- Section 9.2: The CMBT-Method is explained in a nutshell.
- Section 9.3: Describes areas of suggested future studies.

9.1 Summary of the Thesis's Layout

Chapter 1 has introduced the motivation and contribution of the thesis. Then, the research area on which this thesis is built is demonstrated. Chapter 1 ends with the layout of the thesis.

Chapter 2 and 3 respectively provide an in-depth analysis of a wide range of topics such as: Software product lines, Testing software product lines, Variability, Feature modeling, Testing, Quality Assurance, Unified modeling language, Petri Nets, Colored Petri Nets, State Charts, Colored State Charts and embedded reactive systems. This detailed analysis forms a sound background of the area of the research.

Chapter 4 determines more precisely the main requirements of the Colored Model Based Testing for Software Product Lines(CMBT-SWPL) method and what are the steps needed to meet those requirements.

In chapter 5, the example of a Universal Remote Control is used to explain the test method. This example [Die03] was conducted at the Faculty of Computer Science and Automation - Institute of Computer Engineering - Ilmenau University of Technology and it is part of the Digital Video Project(DVP)[Mef03][Str04] based on the VDR project [Gos10].

The main aspects such as Model Based Testing, Statistical Testing, State Charts' Selection to represent behavioral models are explained in chapter 6 in detail to facilitate understanding how testing using the CMBT-SWPL can be applied to the embedded product line domain.

In chapter 7, the Colored State Chart and test method, the Colored Model Based Testing for Software Product Lines(CMBT-SWPL) are presented.

Chapter 8 evaluates the test method and chapter 9 ends with a conclusion and suggested studies.

9.2 CMBT-Method in a Nutshell

In this thesis, a novel approach for the system test of embedded product lines has been presented. Moreover model based testing, which is considered a prerequisite for automated test generation, has been adapted to embedded product lines. The CSC considers variability early in the embedded product line development process and as test cases from CSC automatically are generated, the variability is preserved.

The testing process is divided into two parts:

- Part1: Domain Testing where the following is performed:

    1. Create feature model to capture common and variable features of the product line.

    2. In parallel to the feature model, usage model is developed, represented as a State Chart with usage probabilities.

3. Based on the knowledge captured in the feature model and the previously developed usage model, a customizable statistical test model, namely the Colored State Chart(CSC) is developed. The CSC is linked to all features of the product line by the concept of colors.

4. Out of the domain test model, domain test cases are generated applying statistical testing.

- Part2: Application Testing where the following is performed:

   1. Determine a product line variant, which is a set of features for a specific application to test. Feature model is reused for a specific application (i.e. product line variant.)

   2. Customize the colored domain test model (i.e. one color is chosen) to produce the colored application test model for a specific application based on the selected feature set.

   3. The application CSC is transformed into a State Chart with usage probabilities by removing colors and the corresponding states of unselected features

   4. Out of the application test model, application test cases are generated applying statistical testing.

In addition, the CSC will be transformed to a Colored Petri Net (CPN) for verification and simulation purposes.

9.3 Suggested Studies

The present thesis paves the way for more research work on improving the techniques applied and their tool support.

The applicability and usability of the proposed colors to the test models remain to be investigated in future works for other purposes. For other UML Models, using the concept of colors, will open up new vistas of research areas in testing embedded product lines.

Furthermore, applicability of CMBT-SWPL method on other domains is to be investigated.

Another target is to apply this method in future works to more industrial partners. The aspect of applying this method and integrating it into the Rational Unified Process and with agile methods is the next target. Last but not least the present author hopes that this work will enhance further research.

Synonymic Terminologies

Terminology	Alternate Terminologies
Product Line	Product Family
	Business Unit
Domain Engineering	Software Product Line
	Product Line Development Phase
	Core Asset Development
	Product Line Engineering
	Software Product Line Engineering
	Product Development Preparation Phase
Application Engineering	Product Development
	Actual Product Development Phase
	Product Engineering
Software Core Assets	Platform
	Product Line Infrastructure
	Infrastructure
	Product Line Assets
	Product Line Repository
	Customizable Assets
Product	Customization
	Customized Product
	Application
	Actual Product
	Product Instance

Table 9.1: Synonymic Terminologies

Glossary

Abstraction	Considering certain details and ignoring the rest.
Action	An action is a description of an activity that is to be performed at a given moment.
Application Artifacts	They are the development artifacts of specific product line applications.
Application Design	It is the development of a single application architecture conforming to the reference architecture.
Application Engineering	It is the process in which the applications of the software product line are built by reusing platform artifacts and exploiting the variability of the product line.
Application Realization	It is the development of applications based on the application architecture and the set of domain artifacts.
Application Requirements Engineering	It is the sub-process of application engineering dealing with the communication of product line capabilities to the stakeholders, the elicitation of stakeholder requirements, and the creation of the application requirements specification.
Application Testing	It is the process of uncovering the evidence of defects in a software product line application.
Asset	see development artifact.
Black-box testing	A testing technique whereby the design of tests is based on just the requirements or specification of the system under test, not on knowledge about the implementation of the system.

GLOSSARY

Component	It is a unit of composition with contractually specified component interfaces and explicit context dependencies only; it can be developed independently and is subject to composition by third parties.
Coverage	A measure of how much testing has been done.
Deadlock	A deadlock is a situation where an application locks up because two or more activities are waiting for each other to finish. This occurs in multi-threaded software where a shared resource is locked by one thread and another thread is waiting to access it and something occurs so that the thread holding the locked item is waiting for the other thread to execute.
Development Artifact	It is the output of a sub-process of domain or application engineering. Development artifacts encompass requirements, architecture, components, and tests. Product-line assets. The artifacts are stored in the product-line repository.
Domain	It is an area of process or knowledge driven by business requirements and characterized by a set of concepts and terminology understood by stakeholders in that area. The problem domain and the solution domain are two kinds of domains.
Domain Artifacts	They are reusable development artifacts created in the sub-process of domain engineering. Synonyms are platform and product line artifacts.
Domain Design	It is the development of a reference architecture for the complete software product line.

GLOSSARY

Domain Engineering	It is the process of software product line engineering in which the commonality and the variability of the product line are defined and realized.
Domain Realization	It is the development of the set of reusable components and interfaces within a given reference architecture.
Domain Requirements Engineering	It is the sub-process of domain engineering dealing with the identification of common and variable requirements and their documentation in reusable requirements artifacts.
Domain Test Case	It is a description of a single test flow that has to be performed to test a specific test item. A test case consists of a test case scenario, input data, the expected result, information about the execution, environmental needs, and fail-pass-criteria.
Domain Test Case Scenario	A domain test case scenario is a variable sequence of interactions between variable internal and/or external actors of a system under test.
Error	A human action that produces an incorrect result.
Failure	The symptom of a fault. For example, it is the wrong output, the crash, or the infinite loop that may happen when we execute a fault in the SUT.
Fault	A defect in the SUT. Also known as a bug or an error. When a fault is executed, it may cause a failure.
Feature	It is an end-user characteristic of a system.
Finite State Machine	A model that has a finite number of states and a finite number of transitions between those states.

Formal	Expressed in a notation that can be analyzed automatically, such as a programming language. Contrast to *informal*.
Informal	Expressed in a notation that cannot be analyzed automatically, such as natural language or hand-drawn diagrams. Contrast to *formal*.
JUMBL	The JUMBL is a software tool for statistical testing based on Markov chain usage models developed at the SQRL. Expertise, training, and support is available from Software Silver Bullets.
Livelock	A liveness failure where execution continues endlessly, never reaching an accepting state.
Liveness	The property that something good will happen: execution will reach an accepting state and will avoid dead states, deadlock, and livelock. Or a given scenario will be executed.
Mass Customisation	It is a large-scale production of goods tailored to individual customers' needs.
Model-Based Testing	Model-based testing is a testing technique where the runtime behavior of an implementation under test is checked against predictions made by a formal specification, or model.
Model-based testing	The generation of executable black-box tests from a behavioral model of the SUT.

Operational Profiles	They deal with the use of a system. The user could be a human being or another system that triggers the system under test.
Oracle	A mechanism for analysing SUT output and deciding whether a test has passed or failed.
Product Line Artifacts	see domain artifacts.
Product Management	It is the process of controlling the development, production, and marketing of the software product line and its applications.
Reference Architecture	It is a core software architecture that captures the high-level design of a software product line.
Requirement	It is (1) a condition needed by a user to solve a problem or achieve an objective. (2) A condition or capability that must be met or possessed by a system or system component to satisfy a contract, standard, specification, or other formally imposed document. (3) A documented representation of a condition or capability as in (1) or (2) (IEEE Std 610.12-1990)
Requirement Artifacts	They are products of the requirements engineering process specified using natural language and/or requirements models.
Safety Violations	The program reaches forbidden states.
Scenario	It is a concrete description of system usage, which provides a clear benefit for the actor of the system.

Scoping	It is the process of determining the boundaries of the product line engineering activity. This can be performed on three levels: product portfolio, domain and assets.
Software Architecture	It is the set of the main guiding development principles for one or more software applications. The principles are the solution of one or more architectural concerns dealing with quality.
Software Platform	It is a set of software subsystems and interfaces that form a common structure from which is a set of derivative products can be efficiently developed and produced.
Software Product Line	A collection of applications that have so many features in common that it is worthwhile to study and analyze the common features as well as analyzing the features that differentiate these applications, in order to efficiently develop next generation applications.
State	A current state is determined by past states of the system. As such, it can be said to record information about the past, i.e., it reflects the input changes from the system start to the present moment.
State Chart	A graphical modeling notation that is similar to a finite state machine, but extended with hierarchy of nested states, orthogonal states, and broadcast communication. UML state machines are one example of a State Chart notation.
System Under Test	The program, library, interface, or embedded system that is being tested.

GLOSSARY

Test Artifacts	They are products of the test process containing plans, specifications, and test results.
Test Automation	Test automation is the use of software to control the execution of tests, the comparison of actual outcomes to predicted outcomes, the setting up of test preconditions, and other test control and test reporting functions. Commonly, test automation involves automating a manual process already in place that uses a formalized testing process.
Test case	A sequence of SUT interactions. Each SUT interaction includes the SUT inputs and usually includes the expected SUT outputs or some kind of oracle for deciding whether the actual SUT outputs are correct. When testing nondeterministic SUTs, this view of test cases is sometimes generalized so that a test case is a tree or graph of possible SUT interactions. Note that a test case may be executable (though we usually use the term test script for an executable test case) or may be non-executable because it is a higher level of abstraction than the SUT.
Test driver	A software program that invokes a system under test, provides test inputs to the system, controls and monitors the execution of the tests, and reports test results.
Test script	An executable version of a test case, which is usually written in a programming language, a scripting language, or a tool-specific executable notation.
Test sequence	A synonym for test case.

Test specification	A document in a test plan that specifies the inputs, predicted results, and a set of execution conditions for a test item (IEEE 1998).
Test Suite	A collection of test cases.
Traceability	The ability to trace the connections between the artifacts of the testing life cycle or software life cycle; in particular, the ability to track the relationships between test cases and the model, between the model and the informal requirements, or between the test cases and the informal requirements. Traceability information is often displayed in a traceability matrix.
Traceability Matrix	A table that shows the relationships between two different artifacts of the testing life cycle. For example, the relationships between informal requirement identifiers and generated test cases.
Transition	A transition indicates a state change and is described by a condition that would need to be fulfilled to enable the transition.

GLOSSARY

UML state machine	The Unified Modeling Language has a very rich semantics and notation for describing state machines. UML state machines overcome the limitations of traditional finite state machines while retaining their main benefits. UML state machines introduce the new concepts of hierarchically nested states and orthogonal regions, while extending the notion of actions. UML state machines have the characteristics of both Mealy machines and Moore machines. They support actions that depend on both the state of the system and the triggering event, as in Mealy machines, as well as entry and exit actions, which are associated with states rather than transitions, as in Moore machines.
Use Case	It is a description of system behavior in terms of scenarios illustrating different ways to succeed or fail in attaining one or more goals.
Use case scenario	A sequence of actions that illustrate the execution of a use case instance.
Validation	Determination of the correctness of the products of software development with respect to the user needs and requirements.
Variability mechanism	A technique that enables the representation and automatic configuration of the variability in an application's requirements, models, implementation and tests.
Variant	It is a representation of variability object within domain artifacts.

Verdict	A verdict is the result of an assessment of the SUT correctness. Predefined verdict values are pass, fail, none, and error. Verdict may be computed for a single validation function((n i.e., assertions set), requirement, test case, or entire test.
Verification	The process of evaluating a system or component to determine whether the products of the given development phase satisfy the conditions imposed at the start of that phase.
White-box testing	A box testing technique wherein the design of tests uses knowledge about the implementation of the system (e.g., tests designed to ensure that all statements of the implementation code are tested.

List of Figures

1.1	Defected components and their influence on PL infrastructure	2
1.2	Thesis's Emphasis	3
1.3	Challenges of System Testing in Product Lines	4
1.4	CMBT-SWPL Method	7
1.5	Research Area	8
2.1	Reuse History (adjusted after [Nor08])	10
2.2	A product line from ancient history: The pyramids of Egypt[Gom04] . . .	13
2.3	Platform versus Mass Customization	15
2.4	Product Line Engineering Reference Process	17
2.5	Test Method Extended Product Line Engineering Reference Process . . .	17
2.6	Software Product Lines support Product Diversification	19
2.7	Reuse and MBT - Aspects of comparison	22
2.8	Comparison on Supporting Reuse Or/And Model Based Testing	22
2.9	Colored Model-Based Testing for Software Product Lines(CMBT-SWPL) .	24
2.10	ScenTED (Scenario based TEst Derivation)	26
2.11	Evolutionary Software Product Line Engineering Process merged with CADeT	28
2.12	Testing Strategies for Software Product Lines[JHQJ08]	33
3.1	Different Types of Testing	47
3.2	OO-historie	54
3.3	UML Diagram[OMG09]	55
3.4	Classical Petri Net[vdA10]	56
3.5	Representation of the different States of a State Chart[Mol04]	61
3.6	Representation of the different Transitions of a State Chart[Mol04]	61
3.7	Facts about State Charts 1/3[Amb09][Wik10]	62
3.8	Facts about State Charts 2/3 [Mar05] [Mar09]	63
3.9	Facts about State Charts 3/3 [Mar05] [Mar09]	64

Technical University of Ilmenau

4.1	Main Requirements of CMBT-SWPL Method	73
5.1	Digital Video System Example[SRP03]	76
5.2	Digital Video System Overview[SRP03]	77
5.3	Feature Model for the Universal Remote Control [Die03]	81
5.4	Features in context [Die03]	82
6.1	The W-Model for SPL Test	85
6.2	Model Based Testing	87
6.3	Steps before using the tool JUMBL	94
6.4	A State Chart	95
7.1	Folding of States and Transitions (from [FFDD02])	100
7.2	Example of a Colored State Chart(CSC)	102
7.3	Colored Model-Based Testing for Software Product Lines(CMBT-SWPL) - Domain Engineering	104
7.4	Reduced Feature Model	105
7.5	Product Line Variants to Features Assignments	106
7.6	CSC-Test Model	108
7.7	Product Line Variant1 - v1	109
7.8	Product Line Variant2 - v2	110
7.9	Product Line Variant3 - v3	111
7.10	One product line variant constitute of one or more features	113
7.11	Features to transitions mapping	114
7.12	Test Artifacts	114
7.13	Systematic Test Case Generation	115
7.14	Colored Model-Based Testing for Software Product Lines(CMBT-SWPL) - Application Engineering	116
7.15	Why Statistical Testing?	117
7.16	Statistical Testing based on Usage Models	119
7.17	How is the typical usage obtained?	120
7.18	Petri Net 1	123

7.19	Petri Net 2	124
7.20	Petri Net 3	125
7.21	PENECA Chromos	126
8.1	What makes CMBT-SWPL so special?	129
8.2	CMBT-SWPL Method	131

List of Tables

1.1	Software Product Lines Development	1
2.1	Proactive versus Opportunistic Software Reuse	12
2.2	Domain Engineering Process	14
2.3	Application Engineering Process	15
2.4	Related Work for Software Product Line Testing 1/2	29
2.5	Related Work for Software Product Line Testing 2/2	30
2.6	State-based Software Product Line Testing	31
3.1	Different terms for errors[Kit95]	35
3.2	Historical definitions of testing[Kit95]	40
3.3	Quality Assurance versus Testing[Lew04][Cen07]	42
3.4	Debugging vs. Testing[Bei84]	44
3.5	Black-Box Testing & White-Box Testing	51
9.1	Synonymic Terminologies	137

Bibliography

[AK10] Sven Apel and Christian Kästner. JOT: Journal of Object Technology - An Overview of Feature-Oriented Software Development, 2010. http://www.jot.fm/issues/issue_2009_07/column5/.

[Amb09] Scott Ambler. Introduction to uml 2 state machine diagrams, 2009. http://www.agilemodeling.com/artifacts/stateMachineDiagram.htm.

[Apt10] Aptest. Software testing types, 2010. http://www.aptest.com/testtypes.html.

[Bec00] Kent Beck. *Extreme Programming Explained*. Addison-Wesley, 2000. ISBN 9780201616415.

[Bei84] Boris Beizer. *Software System Testing and Quality Assurance*. Van Nostrand Reinhold, 1984. ISBN 978-1850328216.

[BG04] Antonia Bertolino and Stefania Gnesi. PLUTO: A test methodology for product families. In *Lecture Notes in Computer Science*, pages 181–197, Siena, Italy, 2004. Springer. Accessed: January 2008, http://citeseerx.ist.psu.edu/viewdoc/summary?doi=10.1.1.103.7756.

[BHS99] Kirill Bogdanov, Mike Holcombe, and Harbhajan Singh. Automated Test Set Generation for Statecharts. In *Proceedings of the International Workshop on Current Trends in Applied Formal Method: Applied Formal Methods*, volume 1641, pages 107–121, Boppard, Germany, 1999. Springer. ISBN 978-3540664628.

[BN02] Bart Broekman and Edwin Notenboom. *Testing Embedded Software*. Addison-Wesley, 2002. ISBN 978-0321159861.

[Bob08] Jonas Boberg. Early fault detection with model-based testing. In *Annual ERLANG Workshop archive: Proceedings of the 7th ACM SIGPLAN workshop on ERLANG*, pages 9–20, Victoria, BC, Canada, 2008. ACM. ISBN 978-1-

60558-065-4, http://portal.acm.org/citation.cfm?id=1411276.

[Bos00]   Jan Bosch. *Design and Use of Software Architectures: Adopting and Evolving a Product-Line Approach*. Addison-Wesley Professional, May 29, 2000. ISBN 978-0201674941.

[Cen07]   Resource Center. Software QA and Testing Resource Center, Accessed: December 2007. http://www.softwareqatest.com/.

[CJ02]   Rick D. Craig and Stefan P. Jaskiel. *Systematic Software Testing*. Artech House, 2002. ISBN 978-1580535083.

[CN01]   Paul Clements and Linda M. Northrop. *Software Product Lines : Practices and Patterns*. Addison-Wesley Professional, 3 edition, 2001. ISBN 978-0201703320.

[Die03]   Ralph Dietzel. Konzeption und Entwicklung einer Systemfamilie für eine Universal-Fernbedienung auf Basis eines Palm-Handhelds. Diploma thesis, Technical University of Ilmenau, 2003. Accessd: August 2008, http://www.theoinf.tu-ilmenau.de/ streitdf/DVP/student_work/Ralph_Dietzel/Diplomarbeit.PDF, in German language.

[DM10]   D-MINT. Deployment of model-based technologies to industrial testing, www.d-mint.de, 2010. http://www.dmint.org/, http://www.dmint.de.

[DMMF97]   Bernd Däne, Angela Mölders, Andrea Melber, and Wolfgang Fengler. Modeling an Industrial Transportation Facility with Coloured Petri Nets. In *18th International Conference on Application and Theorie of Petri Nets: Workshop for Manufacturing and Petri Nets*, Toulouse, June 23-27, 1997. Accessed: May 2010, http://tin.tuilmenau.de/ra/ver/, http://tin.tu-ilmenau.de/ra/ver/toul_sld.pdf.

[Dou04]   Bruce Powel Douglass. *Real Time UML: Advances in the UML for Real-Time Systems*. Addison-Wesley Professional, 3 edition, February 27, 2004. ISBN 978-0321160768.

[EFYvB02] Khaled El-Fakih, Nina Yevtushenko, and Gregor von Bochmann. FSM–based Re–Testing Methods. In *TestCom '02: Proceedings of the IFIP 14th International Conference on Testing Communicating Systems XIV*, volume 210, pages 373–390, Deventer, The Netherlands, 2002. Kluwer, B.V. ISBN 0-7923-7695-1.

[Eri03] M. Eriksson. An Introduction to Software Product Line Development. In *Proceedings of Ume's Seventh Student Conference in Computing Science, UMINF-03.05*, pages 26–37, 2003. ISSN 0348-0542.

[Fen93] Wolfgang Fengler. A Coloured Petri Net Interpretation for Modelling and Control in Textile Processing. In *CSCW & Petri Net Workshop, 14th International Conference Application and Theory of Petri Nets*, Chicago, USA, 1993.

[Fen04] Olga Fengler. *Erweiterung und formale Verifikation von dynamischen objektorientierten Modellierungsansätzen auf Basis höherer Petri-Netze*. PhD thesis, Technical University of Ilmenau, 2004. Accessed: August 2008, http://www.db-thueringen.de/servlets/MCRSearchServlet?mode=results&id=xcq7qmw0mi1cgawhyjex&numPerPage=7, in German language.

[FFD02] Olga Fengler, Wolfgang Fengler, and Vesselka Duridanova. Transformation zwischen zustandsorientierten Beschreibungsmitteln der Elektronik und Informatik. *Deutsche Forschungsgemeinschaft: Modelle, Werkzeuge und Infrastrukturen zur Unterstützung von Entwicklungsprozessen. WILEY,VCH&Co. KGaA*, pages 229–245, 2002. in German language.

[FFDD02] Olga Fengler, Wolfgang Fengler, Vesselka Duridanova, and Bernd Däne. Modeling of Complex Automation Systems using Colored State Charts. In *ICRA 2002: Proceedings of the 2002 IEEE International Conference on Robotics and Automation*, volume 2, pages 1901–1906, Washington, D.C, May 2002. IEEE (c) 2002. ISBN 0-7803-7273-5.

[Fow03] Martin Fowler. *UML Distilled: A Brief Guide to the Standard Object Modeling*

Language. Addison–Wesley Professional, 3 edition, September 25, 2003. ISBN 978–0321193681.

[Gee10] Geeks. Difference between Quality Assurance, Quality Control, and Testing, 2010. http://geekswithblogs.net/srkprasad/archive/2004/04/29/4489.aspx.

[GLRW04] Birgit Geppert, Jenny Li, Frank Rößler, and David M. Weiss. Towards Generating Acceptance Tests for Product Lines. In *8th Int'l Conference on Software Reuse. Madrid, Spain*, volume 3107/2004, pages 35–48. Springer Berlin - Heidelberg, 2004. ISBN 978-3-540-22335-1, http://www.springerlink.com/content/c4nytev1vn6c61ch/.

[Gom04] Hassan Gomaa. *Designing Software Product Lines with UML: From Use Cases to Pattern-Based Software Architectures*. Addison-Wesley Professional, Boston, July 17, 2004. ISBN 978-0201775952.

[Gom10] Martin Gomez. Embedded State Machine Implementation, Accessed: January 2010. http://www.embedded.com/2000/0012/0012feat1.htm.

[Gos10] A Gosun. Portal of the video disc recorder project, www.vdr-portal.de, March 2010.

[GTW03] Jerry Zeyu Gao, H.-S. Jacob Tsao, and Ye Wu. *Testing and Quality Assurance for Component-Based Software*. Artech House Publishers, August 31, 2003. ISBN 978-1580534802.

[GvVEB06] Dorothy Graham, Erik van Veenendaal, Isabel Evans, and Rex Black. *Foundations of Software Testing: ISTQB Certification*. CENGAGE Lrng Business Press, 2006. ISBN 1844803554.

[Har87] David Harel. Statecharts: A visual formalism for complex systems. *Science of Computer Programming*, 8(3):231–274, 1987. ISSN 0167-6423.

[HGdR88] C. Huizing, R. Gerth, and W. P. de Roever. Modelling Statecharts Behaviour in a Fully Abstract Way. In *Lecture Notes in Computer Science : CAAP '88*, volume 299/1988, pages 271–294. Springer Berlin - Heidelberg, 1988.

ISBN 978-3-540-19021-9, http://dx.doi.org/10.1007/BFb0026110.

[Hor99] Ian Horrocks. *Constructing the User Interface with Statecharts*. Addison-Wesley Professional, 1 edition, 1999. ISBN 978-0201342789.

[HPR03] Michael Huebner, Ilka Philippow, and Matthias Riebisch. Statistical Usage Testing Based on UML. 2003. Accessed: June 2008, http://www.theoinf.tu–ilmenau.de/ riebisch/home/publ/SCI2003–paper.pdf.

[HS06] Zhaoxia Hu and Sol M. Shatz. Explicit Modeling of Semantics Associated with Composite States in UML Statecharts. *Automated Software Engineering*, 13(4):423–467, October 2006. ISSN 0928-8910 (Print) 1573-7535 (Online).

[HVFR05] Jean Hartmann, Marlon Vieira, Herbert Foster, and Axel Ruder. A UML-based Approach for Validating Software Product Lines. *Innovations in Systems and Software Engineering*, 1(1):12–24, 2005. Accessed: June 2008, http://dx.doi.org/10.1007/s11334-005-0006-0.

[IC08] Ioan Mihnea Iacob and Radu Constantinescu. Testing: First Step towards Software Quality. *Journal of Applied Quantitative Methods*, 3(3), 2008. ISSN 1842-4562, http://jaqm.ro/issues/volume-3,issue-3/4_iacob_constantinescu.php.

[Jen80] Kurt Jensen. A method to compare the descriptive power of different types of petri nets. In *MFCS: Mathematical Foundations of Computer Science 1980*, volume 88/1980, pages 348–361. Springer Berlin - Heidelberg, 1980. ISBN 978-3-540-10027-0.

[Jen97] K. Jensen. A Brief Introduction to Coloured Petri Nets. *Lecture Notes in Computer Science: Tools and Algorithms for the Construction and Analysis of Systems. Proceedings of the TACAS'97 Workshop, Enschede, The Netherlands*, 1217:203–208, 1997. ISBN 3-540-62790-1.

[Jen07] Kurt Jensen. Special section on Coloured Petri Nets. *International Journal on Software Tools for Technology Transfer (STTT)*, 9(3-4):209–212, 2007. ISSN 1433-2779 (Print) 1433-2787 (Online).

[JHQJ08]   Li Jin-Hua, Li Qiong, and Li Jing. The W-Model for Testing Software Product Lines. In *ISCSCT '08: Proceedings of the 2008 International Symposium on Computer Science and Computational Technology*, pages 690–693, Washington, DC, USA, 2008. IEEE Computer Society. ISBN 978-0-7695-3498-5.

[JKB08]   M. Jaring, R.L. Krikhaar, and J. Bosch. Modeling Variability and Testability Interaction in Software Product Line Engineering. In *Seventh International Conference on Composition-Based Software Systems (ICCBSS 2008)*, pages 120–129, Washington, DC, February 25 - 29, 2008. IEEE Computer Society. ISBN 978-0-7695-3091-8.

[Jor97]   Kimberly Jordan. Software Reuse, Term Paper for the MJY Team Software Risk Management WWW Site, 21 April 1997. Accessed: February 2010, www.baz.com/kjordan/swse625/docs/tp-kj.doc.

[JVCS07]   Jonathan Jacky, Margus Veanes, Colin Campbell, and Wolfram Schulte. *Model-Based Software Testing and Analysis with C#*. Cambridge University Press, 1 edition, November 12, 2007. ISBN-13: 978-0521687614.

[KCH+90]   Kyo C. Kang, Sholom G. Cohen, James A. Hess, William E. Novak, and A. Spencer Peterson. Feature-oriented domain analysis (foda), feasibility study. Technical Report CMU/SEI-90-TR-21, ESD-90-TR-222, Carnegie-Mellon University Software Engineering Institute, November 1990.

[Kit95]   Edward Kit. *Software Testing In The Real World: Improving The Process*. Addison-Wesley Professional, 1 edition, November 17, 1995. ISBN 978-0201877564.

[KM04]   Ronny Kolb and Dirk Muthig. Quality Assurance for Software Product Lines. In *Software Product Lines*, volume 3154/2004, pages 84–87. Springer Berlin - Heidelberg, 2004. ISBN 978-3-540-22918-6.

[Kol03]   Ronny Kolb. A Risk-Driven Approach for Efficiently Testing Software Product lines. In *2nd Int'l Conference on Generative Programming and Component Engineering*, Erfurt, Germany, 2003. Accessed: September 2008,

BIBLIOGRAPHY

http://citeseerx.ist.psu.edu/viewdoc/summary?doi=10.1.1.9.3828.

[KPRR03] Erik Kamsties, Klaus Pohl, Sacha Reis, and Andreas Reuys. Testing Variabilities in Use Case Models. In *5th Int'l Workshop on Software Product–Family Engineering*, volume 3014/2004, pages 6–18. Springer Berlin – Heidelberg, Siena, Italy, 2003. ISBN 978-3-540-21941-5, http://citeseerx.ist.psu.edu/viewdoc/summary?doi=10.1.1.85.9264.

[Lar04] Craig Larman. *Applying UML and Patterns: An Introduction to Object-Oriented Analysis and Design and Iterative Development*. Prentice Hall PTR, 3 edition, 2004. ISBN 978-0131489066.

[Lew04] William E. Lewis. *Software Testing and Continuous Quality Improvement*. Auerbach Publications, 2 edition, June 1, 2004. ISBN 978-0849325243.

[LG08] Carlos Luna and Ariel Gonzalez. Behavior Specification of Product Lines via Feature Models and UML Statecharts with Variabilities. In *Proceedings of the 2008 International Conference of the Chilean Computer Science Society*, pages 32–41, Washington, DC, USA, 2008. IEEE Computer Society. ISSN1522-4902, 978-0-7695-3403-9.

[Lim09] M G Limaye. *Software Testing*. Tata McGraw-Hill, Apr-09. ISBN 0070139903.

[Lut07] Robyn Lutz. Survey of Product-Line Verification and Validation Techniques. *FY2007 Software Assurance REsearch Initiative Proposal for the NASA Software IV & V Facility*, May 15,2007. Accessed: June 2008, http://trs-new.jpl.nasa.gov/dspace/bitstream/2014/41221/1/07-2165.pdf.

[Mar05] Peter Marwedel. *Embedded System Design*. Springer, 1 edition, December 14, 2005. ISBN 978-0387292373.

[Mar09] Peter Marwedel. Early design phases, 2009. Accessed: January 2010, http://ls12-www.cs.tu-dortmund.de/staff/marwedel/es-book/slides09/es-marw-2.02-statecharts.ppt.

[McG01] John D. McGregor. Testing a Software Product Line. Technical Report CMU/SEI-2001-TR-022, Software Engineering Institute, Carnegie Mellon University., 2001. Accessed: October 2007, http://www.sei.cmu.edu/library/abstracts/reports/01tr022.cfm.

[McG06] John D. McGregor. Building reusable testing assets for a software product line. In *Reuse of Off-the-Shelf Components*, volume 4039/2006. Springer Berlin - Heidelberg, 2006. ISBN 978-3-540-34606-7.

[Mef03] Florian Meffert. Konzeption einer Videodatenverteilung im Rahmen des Digitalen Video Projektes (DVP). Diploma thesis, Technical University of Ilmenau, 2003. http://www.theoinf.tu-ilmenau.de/streitdf/DVP/student_work/Florian_Meffert/Diplomarbeit.pdf, in German language.

[Met06] Andreas Metzger. Model-based Testing of Software Product Lines. In *Software & Systems Quality Conferences*, Duesseldorf, Germany, May 10 - 12, 2006. Congress Center. Accessed: October 2008, http://www.andreasmetzger.net/pub/MPR06.pdf.

[Mey00] Bertrand Meyer. *Object-Oriented Software Construction*. Prentice Hall, 2 edition, 2000. ISBN 0-13-629155-4.

[Mol04] Maria Mologina. Modellierungstechnik fuer diskrete selbstmodifizierende hard-softwaresysteme. Diploma thesis, Technical University of Ilmenau, 2004. Accessed: March 2008, in German language.

[Mue09] Peter Mueller. Statecharts are real assets! do you know how statecharts can improve software quality?, July 2009. http://www.sinelabore.com/Statecharts_are_real_assets.html.

[Mye04] Glenford J. Myers. *The Art of Software Testing*. Wiley, 2 edition, 2004. ISBN 978-0471469124.

[NFTJ03] Clémentine Nebut, Franck Fleurey, Yves Le Traon, and Jean-Marc Jézéquel. A Requirement-Based Approach to Test Product Families. In *Software Product-Family Engineering: 5th Int'l Workshop,*

BIBLIOGRAPHY

pages 198–210, Siena, Italy, 2003. Springer. Accessed: March 2008, http://citeseerx.ist.psu.edu/viewdoc/summary?doi=10.1.1.83.5110.

[OA99] J. Offutt and A. Abdurazik. Generating Tests from UML Specifications. *UML '99 - The Unified Modeling Language*, 1723/1999, January 01, 1999. ISBN 978-3-540-66712-4.

[OG09] Erika Olimpiew and Hassan Gomaa. Reusable Model-Based Testing. In *Formal Foundations of Reuse and Domain Engineering*, volume 5791/2009, pages 76–85. Springer Berlin - Heidelberg, 2009. ISBN 978-3-642-04210-2.

[Oli08] Erika Mir Olimpiew. *Model-Based Testing for Software Product Lines*. PhD thesis, George Mason University, 2008. Accessed: May 2009, http://hdl.handle.net/1920/3039.

[OMG09] OMG. OMG Unified Modeling Language Specification Version 2.2. 2009.

[PBvdL05] Klaus Pohl, Günter Böckle, and Frank J. van der Linden. *Software Product Line Engineering: Foundations, Principles and Techniques*. Springer Berlin Heidelberg, 1 edition, 2005. ISBN 978-3642063640.

[Poo00] Jesse H. Poore. Introduction to the Special Issue on: Model-Based Statistical Testing of Software Intensive Systems. *Information & Software Technology*, 42(12):797–799, 2000. ISSN: 0950-5849.

[Pro03] S. J. Prowell. JUMBL: A Tool for Model-Based Statistical Testing. *Hawaii International Conference on System Sciences*, 9, 2003. ISBN 0-7695-1874-5.

[Rie03] Matthias Riebisch. Towards a More Precise Definition of Feature Models. In *Modelling Variability for Object–Oriented Product Lines*, pages 64–76. BookOnDemand Publ. Co, 2003. Accessed: November 2007, http://citeseerx.ist.psu.edu/viewdoc/summary?doi=10.1.1.8.9784.

[RKPR05] Andreas Reuys, Erik Kamsties, Klaus Pohl, and Sacha Reis. Model-Based System Testing of Software Product Families. In *Advanced Information Systems Engineering*, volume 3520/2005, pages 519–534. Springer Berlin - Heidelberg,

May 18, 2005. ISBN 978-3-540-26095-0.

[SPH04]   Detlef Streitferdt, Ilka Philippow, and Christian Heller. A component model for applications based on feature models. In *Proceedings of the 2nd Workshop on Software Variability Management - Software Product Families and Populations*, Groningen, December 2004. Accessed: January 2008, http://www.theoinf.tu-ilmenau.de/ streitdf/TheHome/own/data/Groningen_CompModelForFeatureModels.pdf.

[SPR04]   Periklis Sochos, Ilka Philippow, and Matthias Riebisch. Feature-Oriented Development of Software Product Lines: Mapping Feature Models to the Architecture. In *Object-Oriented and Internet-Based Technologies*, volume 3263/2004, pages 138–152. Springer Berlin - Heidelberg, 2004. ISBN 978-3-540-23201-8.

[SRP03]   Detlef Streitferdt, Matthias Riebisch, and Ilka Philippow. Details of formalized relations in feature models using OCL. In *10th IEEE International Conference and Workshop on the Engineering of Computer-Based Systems (ECBS'03)*, pages 297–304, Los Alamitos, CA, US, 2003. IEEE Computer Society. ISBN: 0-7695-1917-2, http://doi.ieeecomputersociety.org/10.1109/ECBS.2003.1194811.

[Str04]   Detlef Streitferdt. *Family-Oriented Requirements Engineering*. PhD thesis, Technical University of Ilmenau, 2004.
http://www.db-thueringen.de/servlets/DerivateServlet/Derivate-2763/ilm1-2004000032.pdf, in German language.

[Tes10]   Model Based Testing, Accessed: March 2010.
http://www.goldpractices.com/practices/mbt/.

[Tri10]   Tripod. What is software testing, Accessed: 2010. http://bazman.tripod.com/.

[Tsa05]   Curtis Tsang. *Object-Oriented Technology from Diagram to Code with Visual Paradigm for UML*. McGraw-Hill, 1 edition, April 26, 2005. ISBN 978-

0073214504.

[UL06] Mark Utting and Bruno Legeard. *Practical Model-Based Testing: A Tools Approach*. Morgan Kaufmann, 1 edition, 2006. ISBN 978-0-12-372501-1.

[Utt06] M. Utting. Position paper: Model-based testing. *Verified Software: Theories, Tools, Experiments (VSTTE)*, 2006. Accessed: March 2009, http://www.cs.waikato.ac.nz/ marku/papers/utting_mbt_position.pdf.

[vdA10] Wil van der Aalst. Petri Nets Refesher. Eindhoven University of Technology, Faculty of Technology Management, Department of Information and Technology, Eindhoven, The Netherlands., Accessed: January 2010. http://wwwis.win.tue.nl/ wvdaalst/workflowcourse/slides/pn2refresher_long.ppt.

[vdLSR07] Frank J. van der Linden, Klaus Schmid, and Eelco Rommes. *Software Product Lines in Action: The Best Industrial Practice in Product Line Engineering*. Springer, 1 edition, July 20, 2007. ISBN 978-3540714361.

[Wik96] D. Wikarski. Petri Net Tools: A Comparative Study. Technical report, ISST-Report Nr. 39. Fraunhofer ISST, Berlin, 1996.

[Wik10] The Free Encyclopedia Wikipedia. Uml state machine, Accessed: February 2010. http://en.wikipedia.org/wiki/UML_state_machine.

[WSS08] Stephan Weißleder, Dehla Sokenou, and Bernd-Holger Schlingloff. Reusing State Machines for Automatic Test Generation in Product Lines. In *1st Workshop on Model-based Testing in Practice (MoTiP 2008)*, Berlin, Germany, Juni 12, 2008. ISBN 978-3-8167-7624-6.

[WT94] James A. Whittaker and Michael G. Thomason. A Markov Chain Model for Statistical Software Testing. In *IEEE Transactions on Software Engineering*, volume 20, pages 812–824. IEEE Press, Piscataway, NJ, USA, 1994. ISSN 0098-5589.

Theses

- The need for a systematic approach for testing becomes more pressing, because of the current trend to increasing complexity and functionality in software product line development.

- Efficient and effective product line testing is crucial to the success of a Software Product Line Engineering (SPLE) in organizations and it depends heavily on establishing the appropriate testing methods.

- Product line test development is of higher complexity than the conventional test development for a single application, given the huge number of applications which can be derived out of the product line.

- Although reuse is a core concept in software product line development, testing has not yet fully benefited from reuse. If not addressed appropriately or addressed late in the development process, testing becomes a serious bottleneck in product line development.

- Software product line testing faces challenges e.g. faces the challenge of variability leading to many applications and the extensive reuse of components, that cannot be tackled by traditional testing techniques. Therefore, testing techniques from the development of single systems have to be adapted and integrated towards a new method.

- A method should be created for developing test models that can mange large numbers of feature combinations.

- Another challenge is the variability in the domain engineering. Each variation point increases the number of possible behaviors to be tested, which makes testing more difficult.

- With early validation testing efforts can be minimized. Accordingly, quality is maintained, which is one aim of software product lines.

- Verification is insufficiently addressed in product lines. The test method suggested consider verification of product lines early.

- Powerful elements and concepts of Colored Petri Nets are adopted in the approach of the Colored State Charts. This helps in diagnosing, tracing and finding errors as it is performed in the Petri Net approach.

- Proactive reuse and the model based testing are two main aspects that should be taken into consideration when testing a software product line.

- Statistical testing is an efficient technique to generate test cases in a systematic way.

- Statistical testing is a technology to reduce the huge test space.

Index

Abstraction, 145
Action, 145
Advantages of State Charts, 101
Ambient Intelligence, 67
Analysing Tool, 127
Application Artifacts, 145
Application Design, 145
Application Engineering, 13, 15, 145
Application Engineering Testing, 121
Application Realization, 145
Application Requirements Engineering, 145
Application Testing, 145
Ariane 5, 39
Asset, 143, 145

Black-Box Testing, 51, 91, 145
Bug, 39

CADeT, 28
Case Study, 77
CMBT-SWPL, 24, 105
Color, 108, 119
Color Transition Function, 109
Color Variable, 109
Colored Petri Net, 55, 58, 127
Colored State Chart, 66, 105
Compact Presentation, 73, 134
Component, 145

Contribution, 6
Core Asset, 143
Coverage, 145
CPN, 127
CSC, 114
D-MINT, 122
Deadlock, 145
Debugging, 44
Defected component, 2
Development Artifact, 145
Digital Video Project, 77
Digital Video System Overview, 79
Domain, 145
Domain Artifacts, 145
Domain Design, 145
Domain Engineering, 13, 14, 145
Domain Engineering Testing, 109
Domain Realization, 145
Domain Requirements Engineering, 145
Domain Test Case, 145
Domain Test Case Scenario, 145

Effective Testing, 46
Embedded Systems, 66
Embedded Systems Characteristics, 67
EPG, 82
Error, 36, 145

Evaluation, 133
Examples of Software Product Lines, 13

Failure, 36, 145
Fault, 36, 145
Feature, 20, 145
Feature Configuration, 110
Feature Model, 81, 83
Feature Modelling, 20
Finite State Machine, 145
Firing, 106, 109
Firing Rule, 109
Folding, 106
Formal, 145
Formal Definitions, 107

GML, 126
Graph Modeling Language, 126

Informal, 145
Informed approach, 96
Infrared Data Association (IrDA) Interface, 80
Infrastructure, 143
Intended approach, 96

JUMBL, 97, 99, 145

Livelock, 145
Liveness, 145

Mapping, 119
Marcov chain, 96
Mass Customisation, 13, 145

Mistake, 36
Model-Based Statistical Testing, 94
Model-Based Testing, 90, 145
Model-Based Testing Steps, 91

Natural Language Specifications, 100

Operational Profiles, 94, 145
Oracle, 145

Palm-Handheld, 80
PENECA Chromos, 127
Petri Net, 55
Phases of Statistical Testing, 96
Platform, 12
PLUS, 28
Probabilities, 123, 126
Product Instance, 143
Product Line Engineering Reference Process, 16
Product Line Repository, 143
Product Line Variant, 113, 115–119
Product Management, 145
Purpose of Testing, 46

Quality Assurance, 35, 41, 42
Quality Control, 41

Rational Unified Process, 90
Reactive Embedded Systems, 69
Reduced Feature Model, 110
Reference Architecture, 145
Related Work, 30, 32
Requirement, 145

INDEX

Requirement Artifacts, 145
Requirements of CMBT-SWPL, 71, 75
Research Area, 8
Reuse, 10

Safety Violations, 145
Scenario, 145
ScenTED, 26
Scoping, 145
Simulation, 59, 127
Software Architecture, 145
Software Platform, 145
Software Product Line, 9, 145
Software Product Line Paradigm, 14
Software Reuse, 10
Software Testing Types, 47
State, 108, 145
State Chart, 60, 99, 145
State-based Software Product Line Testing, 32
Statistical Testing, 94, 122, 123
Statistical Testing using JUMBL, 97
Statistical Usage Testing, 95
Superimposition, 106
Synonymic Terminologies, 143
System Failures, 36
System Testing Challenges, 4
System Under Test, 145
Systematic Test Case Generation, 74

Test Artifacts, 120, 145
Test Automation, 145

Test Case, 145
Test Driven Development, 90
Test Driver, 145
Test Generation, 99
Test Generation using JUMBL, 99
Test Model, 114, 118
Test Process, 45
Test Script, 145
Test Sequence, 145
Test Specification, 145
Test Suite, 145
Testing, 35, 40–42, 44, 45
Testing Benefits, 46
Testing Definition, 40
Testing Principles, 46
Testing Product Lines, 22, 109
Testing Strategies for Software Product Lines, 33
The Model Language, 97
TML, 97, 126
Token, 106
Traceability, 145
Traceability Matrix, 145
Transition, 108, 145
Transition Firing Rule, 109

Ubiquitous Computing, 66
UML state machine, 145
Unified Modeling Language, 52
Uninformed approach, 96
Universal Remote Control, 77

Technical University of Ilmenau

Usage Model, 95, 110, 119

Usage Models, 125

Usage probabilities, 120

Use Case, 145

Use case scenario, 145

Validation, 145

Variability, 16, 19, 73, 100, 119, 134, 138, 140

Variability mechanism, 145

Variant, 145

VDR project, 77

Verdict, 145

Verification, 60, 127, 136, 145

W-Model, 87, 89

W-Model for Testing Software Product Lines, 87

White-Box Testing, 51, 145

Die VDM Verlagsservicegesellschaft sucht für wissenschaftliche Verlage abgeschlossene und herausragende

Dissertationen, Habilitationen, Diplomarbeiten, Master Theses, Magisterarbeiten usw.

für die kostenlose Publikation als Fachbuch.

Sie verfügen über eine Arbeit, die hohen inhaltlichen und formalen Ansprüchen genügt, und haben Interesse an einer honorarvergüteten Publikation?

Dann senden Sie bitte erste Informationen über sich und Ihre Arbeit per Email an *info@vdm-vsg.de*.

Sie erhalten kurzfristig unser Feedback!

VDM Verlagsservicegesellschaft mbH
Dudweiler Landstr. 99   Telefon +49 681 3720 174
D - 66123 Saarbrücken   Fax   +49 681 3720 1749
www.vdm-vsg.de

Die VDM Verlagsservicegesellschaft mbH vertritt

MIX
Papier aus verantwortungsvollen Quellen
Paper from responsible sources
FSC® C105338

Printed by Books on Demand GmbH, Norderstedt / Germany